PASTOR'S CASEBOOK

OTHER BOOKS BY JOHN LANCASTER

The Spirit Filled Church
In Spirit and In Truth
Your Guide to the Christian Life

PASTOR'S CASEBOOK

by John Lancaster

Published by: Elim Publications Board
Elim Pentecostal Church,
P. O. Box 38,
CHELTENHAM.

 ISBN: 0 905857 03 8

DEDICATION

To Tim and Sue, Andy and Beth, in appreciation of your patience in sharing me with a much larger family, and for the love and laughter that has contributed so much to a happy home.

CONTENTS

INTRODUCTION

When David Winter, then Editor of *CRUSADE* magazine, first invited me to write a series of articles based on a pastor's experiences I hesitated. For one thing I was anxious not to betray the confidences reposed in me and for another I was afraid that the stories might tempt people who know me to "spot the characters" in real life. I felt the same hesitation when the present book was suggested and it was only after some gentle arm twisting I agreed to its publication.

A number of the stories have already appeared in *CRUSADE* and I am grateful to the present Editor for his permission to reprint them. My thanks go also to Gordon Stowell for his kind permission to reproduce some of the illustrations which added interest to the original series, and to David Wright for his fine drawings.

It should be clearly understood that the names and locations in the stories are entirely fictitious. Most of the locations described are areas in which I have never ministered, other than as a visiting preacher. The stories are based on real incidents but the actual details in each case and most of the dialogue are fictitious.

It would be most unfair if the impression was gained that the stories represent the kind of people who made up the congregations to which I have ministered during the last thirty years. The vast majority of those people have been good, solid Christians whose love and helpfulness have sustained me in my ministry and to whose steadfastness I gladly pay tribute. The people in these pages are to be found in every church – and rightly so; for the Church exists not as a club for the spiritually perfect but as a home for sinners saved by grace, in which loving, caring, sharing and learning are all part and parcel of life.

The stories follow no strict chronological order but are simply chosen to illustrate the kind of problems which confront the pastor and his church when they make themselves available to people in a troubled world. This book is in no sense intended as a "guide to counselling" – specialists in that field will swiftly spot its weaknesses - but is rather the record of one pastor's experiences, "warts and all", which may be of some help to others.

I am sorry that the constant use of the personal pronoun has been necessary to the narrative form of these chapters and hope it is not unduly obtrusive. My hope is that by sharing these real-life experiences others may be encouraged to see that the ministry of the local church is achieved not so much by professional techniques as by Christ's love shed abroad in our hearts, moving us with compassion and constraining us to take time to listen and share in the needs of others.

John Lancaster

There is a tide ...

The dying light of a December sun brought a faint flush of pink to the otherwise grey and deeply furrowed face of a cloudy sky. The stark, jagged timbers of a rotting barge rose out of the gleaming waters of the deserted dock like the massive ribs of some long-dead sea monster, while in striking contrast a swan moved across the greyness with a tranquil white elegance. In the distance six great cranes lifted their necks against the sky like huge skeletal giraffes waiting to gorge themselves on their next victim, and through the gathering mists of late afternoon the deep-throated blare of a ship's siren rolled across the town towards the distant hills.

For a moment or two I paused on my way home from an afternoon's visiting to watch the changing patterns of light and shade on the receding tide, and then I noticed a familiar figure leaning on the railings some distance away. With one foot on the lower rail, Bill Faraday leaned on his forearms, clasping his hands together and thrusting his head forward as though he had seen something unusual on the far side of the dock.

"Hullo Bill", I said, walking over to where he stood, "what have you spotted?"

He started a little at my greeting, and then smiled. "As a matter of fact, I've been doing a bit of quiet thinking", he said.

For a few moments we stood together in silence watching the small boats swing at their moorings as the ebb tide slid from under them, and then Bill drew in a deep breath.

"I haven't said anything to anyone about this, Pastor", he said slowly, "but I think God is calling me to the mission field" He threw me a quick glance as though to judge my reaction and then went on. "The trouble is, I don't want to go! I'm happy in my work, I've got all my friends here in the church, and what's more mum and dad are getting on now and they need me around to keep an eye on things, Besides, the thought of having to go to Bible college scares me – I've never been much good as book-learning". He paused again. "And yet", he said with a sigh, "I can't get away from this feeling that God wants me to go".

"Lord", I prayed inwardly, "help me to say the right thing to Bill". My mind went back to the two ministers who had particularly helped me in this matter: the one who had warned me, when I confided to him my youthful ambition to become a minister, that without the certainty of God's call I would make the greatest mistake of my life; and the one who recognised that God *had* called me *and* helped me to fulfil that calling when the right time had come. I remembered, too, the young people who had come to me after some moving service, assuring me that God had called them to be missionaries or ministers, so often to prove in the weeks or months that followed that the "call" was but an echo of a passing emotion.

I asked Bill how he had "felt called". It seemed that a few months earlier he had become aware of a growing inner conviction that God was calling him. There were no special circumstances, no lights or voices or unusual emotional experiences, just a steadily growing awareness that God wanted him. Certain scriptures from his daily Bible readings seemed to speak with special force, and then the visit from a missionary to the church crystallised everything. Yet still he hesitated.

"You know, Bill", I said, after he had told me his story, "in some ways it is a good thing to hesitate. The Lord himself warned us about the need to count the cost before accepting the challenge of His service, and some of the greatest of God's servants – Moses, Isaiah, Jeremiah – were very hesitant about entering his work". I told him of the warning I had received and how in later years I had proved its truth. "There have been times, Bill, when the only thing that has kept me going in the work of God has been the fact that I knew without a shadow of doubt that God had called me".

Bill nodded. "I realise that once the glamour has worn off, missionary work is hard and tedious. It looks all right on coloured slides, but it must be pretty tough when you're out there year after year".

I laid my hand on his arm. "Bill", I said, "the work of God is sometimes very hard, but it is also very wonderful. It means sacrifice, but it also means the greatest joy in the world – the joy of working together with God for the salvation of men". I promised him that I would pray with him that God would show him very clearly that He had called him, and I reminded him that if God *had* called him then He would also deal with the matter of his responsibilities at home and his anxiety about Bible college.

By now the light had faded and the reflections of the street lamps danced on the dark waters below us, and as Bill turned to go I realised with an uncomfortable feeling that if God had really called him He was removing one of my key youth workers. For a moment I hesitated. Perhaps I should dissuade him. After all, he was doing a great job of work amongst the needy youngsters of the dockland area. In fact, he *was* a missionary already! What would I do without him? Who was there to replace him? The arguments crowded in on me, and then suddenly my own words came back to me like a boomerang – "If God has called you, then He will deal with the problems His call creates . . .". The distant call of a ship nosing her way out to the open sea came to my ears, and in the darkness I could still see the little boats straining at their moorings, yearning to go with the tide, and deep in my heart I knew that the call of the tide must be obeyed.

"When you're absolutely sure God has called you, Bill", I said, "come back and tell me".

Some time later Bill came, and soon afterwards he was accepted as a candidate for missionary training. God provided for his ageing parents in a wonderful way. One of the members of the church made them his special care, feeling that this was a practical way in which he could help forward the work of God in other lands, and although we found Bill hard to replace in our youth work we eventually discovered some hidden talent amongst our congregation and so the gap was filled. Bill's first vacation from college showed the results from training. To his enthusiasm had been added deeper understanding and a new confidence. It was not until his last year of training that I noticed a difference in him. At first I put this down to the listlessness which comes to many students as they approach the end of their training, but a talk with Bill made me realise that there were other reasons.

I had asked him to come visiting with me, feeling that the experience might help him, and our last call had taken us to a housing estate which overlooked the town. As we emerged from one of the top floor flats we paused to admire the view from the balcony, Below us the town arched in a crescent of blue and red roofs, from which tall chimneys and church spires rose amidst clusters of trees and twisting roadways. Beyond the smoke haze stood the wharves and cranes of the docks, and out on a shimmering sea busy tugs hurried officiously towards an incoming liner. I nodded towards the distant ship.

"It hardly seems possible that you'll be setting sail before very much longer", I said.

Bill hesitated, then cleared his voice. "I wonder", he said softly.

I looked at him in surprise. His face was drawn and set, and a small muscle in his cheek moved nervously. "What's wrong, Bill?" I asked.

For a moment he didn't answer. Then he rubbed his

forefinger over his eyebrow. "To tell you the truth", he said, "I feel all mixed up. The nearer I get to the mission field, the more afraid I feel. When I first went to college I was full of enthusiasm and everything was fine – and I've certainly done better in the exams than I thought I would – but it's . . . well, I just don't feel sure of myself any more. When I think of the responsibilities I shall have to carry and the type of work I shall be expected to do I feel so inadequate, and I begin to wonder if I haven't made an awful mistake".

He fell silent and I realised that he was deeply troubled by this sense of personal inadequacy. "You know, Bill", I said, "in a situation like this there is one basic question that needs to be faced before you can go any further".

He turned quickly and said, "What's that?" And the eagerness with which he said it revealed his desperate longing to get things sorted out.

"Well", I said, "the first thing you must ask yourself is, 'Am I reasonably certain that I am in God's will?' " I explained why I said "reasonably certain". In the matter of knowing God's will, I had discovered in my own life and in the lives of others that there were times when a glib assumption had passed for a real assurance, and because of this I had grown less dogmatic about the will of God. "On the other hand", I assured him, "I do believe that when we sincerely seek to know God's will He does definitely reveal it to us. It may be through the Bible, or an inner conviction, or the overruling of circumstances, or more possibly through the combination of several converging lines of evidence, but whenever we humbly and obediently seek to know His will God will make it clear . . .".

Before I could continue Bill broke in. "That's the funny thing, you see. I still feel that God called me, and I don't feel that I have stepped out of His will in going to college – it's just that I feel so uncertain about my ability to do the job".

"Look, Bill", I said, "if you can feel reasonably certain

that you are doing what God wants you to do, you can also be certain that He will enable you to do it". God, I reminded him, doesn't make a mistake when He chooses men – He knows what is in man, and He knows the possibilities of every life that is yielded to His control. I reminded him again of how diffident Moses had been and of the excuses he had made for not doing God's will. But his own autobiography proved him wrong. I pointed him to God's word to Paul: "My grace is sufficient for you: for my strength is made perfect in weakness". I confided to him that not only at the beginning of a man's ministry but right the way through there were times when an appalling sense of personal inadequacy faces him. "You see, Bill, just as an eagle forces her young out of the comfort of the nest so that they may exercise their wings and so realise their true environment, so God sometimes puts us in a position where we feel so inadequate that we are driven to exercise faith and prayer in a new way. In this way our latent powers are brought into play and our moral muscles are strengthened, but more than this, we are forced back on God in a deeper way and so through our weakness His strength is made perfect in us".

Eventually we made our way back to the car, and as we parted we covenanted to pray that God would confirm His will for Bill's life. The confirmation came and eventually the day when Bill set sail. I stood waving as his ship eased away from the quay with its escort of screeching gulls. The mighty blast of her siren rang in my ears, recalling that grey December afternoon when Bill had first disclosed his sense of God's call. I thought again of the small boats tugging at their moorings, and I remembered how reluctant Bill had been to launch out into the deep. Now he was on his way, a small figure waving goodbye as the great ship caught the tide.

"There is a tide in the affairs of men", I thought to myself, "and for Bill it's the tide of God's great purpose".

It isn't always cricket ...

Crack! The delicious sound of a well-struck ball echoed across the park, followed by a cry of "Hurry up, Ginger!" The object of this exhortation came panting towards me in the wake of a swiftly rolling cricket ball. I stopped the ball with my foot and tossed it to the tousle-haired youngster who took it gratefully and then tried to throw it to the wicket keeper. The throw was not very successful and in the interval while another fielder fetched the ball, Ginger turned his attention to me.

"Hullo Sir", he said politely.

"Hullo", I said, "haven't I seen you before somewhere?" The rather pimply face looked familiar.

"Yeah", he said, with a vigorous nod of the head, "down at your Sunday school. I've just started to come with me mate". He looked at me for a moment, as if running an expert eye over my physical condition. "Here", he said, jerking his thumb over his shoulder towards the stumps, "want a game?"

Finding a cricket ball hard to resist, I joined in for a while and then as the shadows of the poplars stretched themselves on the turf, as though settling down for the night, we made our way homeward across the park. At the gates Ginger waved his hand in farewell. "See you", he said.

"See you", I answered.

And see him I did, more than I expected.

Ginger had started Sunday school late in life. He was already fourteen when his mate, Stephen, had coaxed him to come, but he seemed to have settled down in the boys' Bible class quite quickly. A little later I was glad to see his shock of red hair amongst a group of less distinguished heads bent over a project in one of our week-night youth groups. And when I commented on the fact, John Gray, the youth leader involved with the group, told me that Ginger seemed to be showing a genuine interest in the spiritual side of things. "He could go far, that lad, if he gets the right help", John said.

It was John who identified the stranger sitting with Ginger in one of our Sunday evening services some months later.

"Did you see the big man with Ginger tonight?" he asked excitedly.

"Yes", I said, "I did, but unfortunately I wasn't able to speak to him. Old Mrs. Grimble cornered me over some trifling matter and I couldn't get to speak to several people I wanted to have a word with".

"I know exactly how you feel", John said. "Some people live on trifles – that's why they're so thin!" He grinned at me as if willing me to laugh at his somewhat feeble attempt at wit. "Anyhow, the chap with Ginger tonight was his father. I managed to have a word with him and he said he'd enjoyed the service and would be coming again".

"Good", I said, although inwardly I wondered whether people who said they'd 'enjoyed it' were really telling the truth, and if they were, whether the Gospel had been successfully communicated to them. After all, I don't suppose Felix said he'd enjoyed the meeting after Paul had preached to him about righteousness, self-control and judgment to come. Suddenly I became aware of John looking at me questioningly. "Sorry", I said, "I was just thinking".

It must have been about a fortnight after this that Ginger's father came to the vestry after the Sunday evening service. He eased himself into the chair opposite me and spread large hands over his knees. He was a large man altogether, tall and chubby with at least three stubby chins to his round florid face. A thin grey moustache followed the contours of his upper lip, matching the well-greased hair which was brushed back from his fairly high forehead. His suit had a much 'lived in' look but otherwise he was reasonably tidy. For a moment he was silent, then running a hand over his hair he said in a gravelly voice, "Well . . . I think I'd like to join your church".

This surprised me, because I had not felt that his few appearances at church had had much effect on him. Rather, I felt he had come merely to please Ginger. However, I talked with him for some time and tried to explain that becoming a member of a church did not necessarily make one a Christian.

"You see", I said, "there are plenty of church members who are not Christians at all, because being a Christian means much more than merely going to church; it means repenting of your sin and turning in faith to Christ and personally receiving Him as your Saviour and then being willing to follow Him as a humble disciple".

He listened intently, his grey-green eyes hardly shifting their gaze from me, and when at length I invited him to pray he seemed willing. Afterwards he rose from his knees, pulled his crumpled jacket straight and then offered me his hand. "Thank you", he said as we shook hands, "I'm sure that will help a lot".

I watched him amble from the room holding the literature I had given him, to all intents and purposes a new convert; but in the back of my mind the dorsal fin of a niggling doubt broke surface and troubled the waters. How hard it is to really know the truth about men; how often human wisdom and experience only touch the surface. It takes the insight of the Holy Spirit to truly read the hearts of men. "O Lord", I prayed that night, "grant me greater wisdom and understanding in dealing with men".

In some ways I was not surprised when a few weeks

later Ginger's father rang me up. He wanted my advice, and could he call round and see me. I agreed and within minutes he was at the house. He sat down slowly and then scratched the back of his head. I noticed his eyes were avoiding mine.

"Well . . . I'm afraid this is a bit awkward", he began, "but I'm sure you'll be able to help—even if only for Reggie's sake".

For a moment I hesitated, then I remembered that Reggie was Ginger's more official name.

"How can I help?"

He cleared his throat and then unfolded his story. His wife had died from cancer when Reggie was only small but he had struggled to bring up the lad. It wasn't easy, but neighbours and relatives had helped as far as looking after the boy was concerned. Of course, now he was older that didn't matter so much, but he still had to be fed and clothed and there was the rent to find. Anyhow, he had got into debt through being ill and off work, and he had been tempted. "It was easy, see", he said hoarsely, "I was left on me own a good bit down at the works and nobody would know what I was doing. Leastways, that's what I thought, but somehow or other they got on to me and I'm in a proper mess now".

It seemed that he had been 'pinching stuff', to put it in his own words, and had been found out and summoned to appear before the magistrates. What he wanted to know was whether I would be willing to speak on his behalf. Questioning him further, I began to realise the real reason for his 'conversion'. That had been the weekend he knew he'd been found out. I was tempted to be angry at the deception, but then I remembered the patience of God and also the fact that young Ginger was involved in all this. I promised to help.

My good intentions received a further blow in court when I learned that this was the second occasion such a thing had happened. A detective sergeant gabbled his oath in a hurried blur of words and then gave his evidence, which included an uncomplimentary description of the home in which this unhappy man and his son lived. Then I found myself confronting an elderly magistrate who peered at me disbelievingly through his bifocals. Reggie was behind my plea for lenience. The magistrate was not so sure. He had, to my way of thinking, some unnecessarily harsh things to say about the man in the dock, but after the diatribe he gave him two years' probation.

It must have been early January the following year when it all came back to me. John Gray was about to leave the house after a committee meeting when he turned and said, "By the way, what did you think about the test match?"

"Very good", I said, "the Aussies take some beating on their own grounds". Then I stopped. Cricket! The delicious feeling when you've hit the ball with the meat of the bat. Crack! "Hurry up, Ginger!" . . . Ginger . . . Ginger's dad . . . an oak panelled courtroom . . . light glinting on bifocals, an elderly voice churning out official displeasure.

"Have you seen anything of Ginger lately?" I asked John.

"No, not for a while. It's a pity. I thought at one time we might have been able to do something with him. But, tell me, what's the test match got to do with Ginger?" John Gray looked at me with a puzzled frown.

I explained how I'd first met Ginger during a game of cricket.

"You know", I said, "I really thought that something would have come out of that, it seemed as if some divine plan was unfolding, especially when his dad became interested as well. Yet, after all we tried to do for them, neither of them come near the place now. In fact, when I met his father in the street a couple of weeks ago he just ignored me. Life's a strange thing".

John nodded. "It certainly is, and it isn't always cricket".

The restless one ...

My lips were saying, "And now let us think about the personal implications of our text . . ." but my mind was whispering fiercely, "What's wrong with Daniel Redman?" It was Sunday evening. The soft rosy light of the setting sun flooded in through the chapel windows, gleaming on the varnished pews and the decorative gilt on the organ pipes and shedding a mellow glow on the rows of upturned faces beneath the high pulpit from which I was preaching. Mr. Idris Powell's gold-rimmed spectacles glinted as he looked up from his Bible, and the diamond pin in Mrs. Rees-Evans' summer hat flashed as she moved to a more comfortable position, but apart from the clatter of young Tommy Pugh's dropped pencil and the fidgetting of some of the other children on this warm summer's evening the congregation was listening intently—all, that is, except Daniel Redman. Daniel was thumbing through the pages of his hymn book in a way which seemed to be saying, "Look, Pastor, I'm not interested in what you've got to say, so don't kid yourself!" The hunch of his shoulders and the expression on his face indicated studied boredom. And my mid-sermon impression was strengthened by the fact that Daniel was not playing his piano accordian at the young peoples' squash after the service.

As it happened, I ran into Daniel the following afternoon. He stepped out of a house in Llewellyn Street as I was making my way to the local hospital. By the time he had made an entry in his insurance book I had reached him. He looked up as I greeted him.

"Afternoon, Pastor", he said cheerfully, "lovely day!"

I nodded. "Even Llewellyn Street looks pleasant on a day like this", I said. We both looked down the long curve of the street to where the unbroken line of grey stone houses ended and the three ancient petrol pumps of Morgan's Garage stood staring brazenly across the road at the crumbling facade of Siloah Independent Chapel. Beyond the chapel rose the green slopes of the mountain, and a little group of brightly clad children was climbing a well worn path towards the top. Daniel snapped his insurance book shut.

"Must be nice up there this afternoon", he said, "but there, some of us have to work for our living. I wish I was a kid again sometimes".

Something in his tone of voice confirmed my feeling that all was not well with him. "You sound more like Nebuchadnezzar than Daniel", I said laughingly. There was no smile on his face, however. Instead he kicked an empty cigarette packet into the gutter.

"Oh, I don't know", he said, "nothing ever seems to change in this dump". He narrowed his eyes against the glare of the sun as he stared down the street. "Everybody seems in a rut. There's nobody with vision, nobody willing to face the facts. Everybody seems so self-satisfied. We sing the same hymns, listen to the same people praying, we do the same things week in, week out. There's no life, no power, no blessing. And it's always the same people who do everything". Having delivered this outburst he glanced suddenly at his watch and exclaimed, "Anyway, I must be off! Be seeing you". He turned to go, but as he did so I laid my hand on his arm.

"I mustn't keep you from your work, Daniel", I said, "but I'd like you to look in and have a chat with me when we've both got more time. And, by the way, do you remember what Shakespeare said?" He looked puzzled and shook his head. I repeated for him the well-worn lines:

"The fault, dear Brutus, is not in our stars, but in ourselves, that we are underlings". He still looked puzzled as he walked off, and to judge from the way the lace curtains moved in old Mrs. Thomas's front window I guessed she was puzzled too. "There's funny! The Pastor quoting Shakespeare to that young Daniel Redman in the street. On Monday afternoon, too!"

If my conversation with Daniel had seemed lighthearted it was not due to a lack of concern for him. Some people are spiritual hypochondriacs, having regular bouts of excessive anxiety about their own or other people's spiritual health and to take such people too seriously is sometimes to aggravate their condition. However, I was concerned about Daniel and in the quietness of my study I prayed for him and considered the best means of helping him. I liked him, but he troubled me. He was a young man with considerable gifts yet somehow he had never taken his place in the life of the church as we had hoped. I remembered old Tom Edwards, the boy's Bible class leader, nudging me in the ribs with his bony elbow and confiding to me in a wheezy whisper, "That boy's got promise, Pastor. A bit of a lad at times, mind you, but knows his Bible he does, and knows how to put things together too". Old Tom was right. Daniel *was* promising. But as I mused I realised that it takes more than Bible knowledge and a fluent tongue to make a good Christian worker. A steady, dependable Christian character is sometimes of more value than many talents.

The trouble with Daniel, it seemed to me, was that he was unwilling to accept the down to earth facts of Christian discipleship. He would come back from some convention full of enthusiasm. For a week or two he would be at every meeting and ready to accept any assignment, and then gradually the fire would burn down until the next wind of enthusiasm stirred the smouldering embers.

We had tried giving him opportunities for Christian service but so far this had not proved very successful. I recalled that he had volunteered to become a Sunday school teacher and was assigned a class, but that experiment had lasted only a few weeks because he had been unwilling to use the prescribed teacher's handbook. "I believe in the liberty of the Spirit, not in man-made systems", he had told the Superintendent; and no amount of reasoning could persuade him differently. Then there was the time he had been made secretary of one of our youth groups. We had wondered why that particular group was losing ground, until we discovered that Daniel was often absent on the meeting night. When I spoke to him about this he explained that he had been away speaking at other meetings, and when I pointed out that his duty was to be in the place for which he had accepted responsibility he became belligerent and said he believed in being led by the Spirit, not being in bondage to "organised religion". There was a restlessness in Daniel that worried me. He seemed to be always seeking for excitement, always dashing off to conventions and special meetings, always craving for a fresh shot of spiritual stimulant to pep up his jaded soul. He was a meeting-addict, a spiritual "restless one".

Eventually he came to see me. I took him into the room which served me as a study and bedroom and my landlady, Mrs. Harris, brought us tea. For a while I let him talk. Slowly at first and then with increasing passion he unburdened himself. He had been up the valley to some wonderful meetings. He told me of the fervour and freedom he found there and then proceeded to contrast all this with what he felt was wrong with his own church. The deacons, the members of the church, the other young people and the activities of the church all came in for devastating treatment, and though he didn't name me I felt pretty sure that I was just about top of his list. "Nothing but a mighty revival will do any good", he said sternly, "but I doubt if many of them up there are prepared for it".

While he had been talking I had walked to the window and had suddenly seen something that gave me a clue. I called him to my side and together we looked over the jumble of streets and factories, schools and churches which made up this typical mining town. I pointed beyond the distant slag heaps and mine workings to where the brown waters of the river curved in a gentle sweep through the fields. "I suppose you used to play in the river when you were a lad, Daniel", I said.

He looked at me uncertainly, trying to discover the connection between that remark and his own spate of words. "Well, actually my father wouldn't allow me to play there", he said. "You see, before the hydro-electric installation was built a lot of these rivers were quite fast and dangerous. They're not so bad now".

I nodded. "You know", I said, "you remind me of that river, Daniel! You're full of energy and enthusiasm, sometimes you're fast and furious, but so far you haven't got very far–and what is more you never will until you are willing to let God harness your life and control its energies". Gently but firmly I took him back over his life, making him see how he had rebelled against the necessary discipline of the Christian life. I pointed out to him that real spiritual growth was not so much from the stimulation of special meetings, however good, but from the steady discipline of a personal walk with God in prayer and obedience to His Word. And real usefulness in God's service, I reminded him, comes through the discipline of a well-ordered church life. The church is the Body of Christ, I pointed out, and unless the individual members of that Body are willing to live and move and work together the Body can never function properly.

"Sometimes the church is called to unspectacular and unexciting tasks", I said, "but if its members are faithful and loyal to God and each other then Christ is able to achieve His purpose through it". I directed his gaze to the river again. "Just as those waters have been harnessed and are now producing power and light, so you must let God discipline and harness your life if it is to become really effective".

For once Daniel had nothing to say, but through the

ensuing months he sought to accept the principles I had endeavoured to teach him. He didn't find it easy but gradually the results began to show in the steady consistency of his life and service. Some time later he came to me, Bible in hand. "I'm preparing a sermon about our need of God's control in our lives", he said, "and I'm trying to find a text you once quoted about 'the fault is in ourselves', or something like that".

I smiled. "You won't need a concordance for that one, Daniel", I said. "Try Shakespeare!"

How black was my valley ...

Ted Wetherby proffered his battered black Homburg to the crowd with the air of a man parting with his most cherished possession.

"Friends", he croaked hoarsely, "Salvation is a free gift!"

Most of Ted's 'friends' looked unimpressed. They had been with him a long time—too long, in fact, and, for all his undoubted earnestness, he hadn't succeeded in making the Christian faith any more exciting than his black Homberg. Noting the crowd beginning to drift away, I tiptoed quietly round the ring to where Hugh Fellowes stood. A gifted speaker with a passionate concern for people, Hugh always seemed able to draw and hold the crowd. I touched him on the arm.

"Hugh", I whispered, "will you have a word next?"

He hesitated, and then whispered back, "I'd rather not tonight".

A little surprised at his reluctance, since usually in the open air he was like a hound straining at the leash, I pressed him further but he shook his head emphatically and there I had to leave it. He slipped off quickly after the meeting, but I paid little attention to the incident, attributing his reluctance to some minor cause. It was only when he had been absent from the next couple of open air meetings that I began to wonder whether there was some more serious reason.

When Sunday came I managed to catch him after the morning service just as he had mounted his scooter.

"Hugh", I said, "is everything all right? I've missed you from the open airs recently".

The spluttering engine died away to an inoffensive cackle as he eased the throttle. "Can't stop now, Pastor, but I'd like to have a word with you some time", he said, and with that he fastened the clip on his helmet and drove off.

The following Friday Mrs. Harris, my kindly landlady, asked the inevitable question: "Have you got to go out tonight, Pastor?"

With a flourish I took out my diary.

"Mrs. Harris", I said light heartedly, "look – no meeting, no committee, no visiting. In fact, nothing to do and all night to do it in!"

Mrs. Harris eyed me suspiciously and her lilting voice had a slightly higher pitch than usual.

"There's nice for you", she said, "and what time would you like your supper?"

The prospect of a night off was indeed pleasant. I sank back into an old but very comfortable arm chair and while the fire licked at a fresh log like a dog with a new bone I relaxed with a travel book about Burma. The warmth of the fire and the vivid description of places made familiar through war service carried me far away from the dark, rain-swept streets of the mining town which was now my home, but suddenly what might have been the tinkling of pagoda bells resolved itself into the sound of Mrs. Harris's front door chimes, and footsteps on the stairs confirmed my fears that what was to have been a night off was about to be switched on. A few seconds later a knock on the door announced the arrival of Hugh Fellowes.

"I'm sorry to trouble you", he said, as I motioned him to a chair by the fire, "but I felt I must come".

"That's all right", I said, nodding assent to Mrs. Harris's silent query from the door as to whether she should make the inevitable cup of tea. "As a matter of fact I thought of coming to see you tonight, but then I remembered you usually go up the valley to see your mother on Friday nights".

Hugh had pulled off his large leather gauntlets and was now sitting forward in his chair polishing his glasses with his handkerchief.

"Yes, I usually do", he said, "but I felt I must come and see you tonight".

The fire light threw into sharp relief the well-defined contours of his face, emphasising the straightness of his nose, the hollows of his deep-set eyes with their dark, bushy brows, and the mobile mouth which gave one the impression of eloquence even before he spoke. He slid his glasses back into place and then ran his hand over his dark, slightly wavy hair, and as I watched him I sensed that he was a very troubled man.

Hugh was a teacher at one of the local secondary modern schools, specialising in English. A young man of wide interests, he combined an enthusiasm for music and drama with a passion for rugby, but there was also a vibrant spiritual quality about him which gave added strength to a naturally energetic character. It was unusual to see him so subdued, and while he paused before explaining why he had come to see me I offered a silent prayer for God's help.

Slowly and thoughtfully Hugh described what was troubling him, his rich voice unusually hesitant. Until a few months ago, it seemed, life had been full and immensely satisfying. During the summer holidays he had taken a group of his boys to camp and had seen several of them receive Christ and this in turn had opened the way for a Christian fellowship in the school. New opportunities came his way and during the first weeks of the autumn term he had never enjoyed his Christian experience so much. Then gradually and almost imperceptibly a spiritual decline had set in. Prayer became difficult, Bible reading a duty rather than a delight and the zest went out of life.

"That's one reason why I didn't want to speak in the

open air the other afternoon", he said quietly, "but there's something else, too. You see, I've found myself becoming so critical of others. I find myself in the prayer meeting finding fault with people's grammar and getting impatient with their mistakes instead of really entering into the meeting. I suppose I was fed up with old Ted Wetherby rambling on in that open air and didn't want to be part of it". He paused and sighed, and then with an expansive gesture went on. "I feel as though I'm in some deep dark valley and there's no way out. The more I try to pray and read the Bible, the harder things seem to get".

He fell silent, and for a few moments the only sound was the clatter of rain on the window pane.

"You know, Hugh", I said after a while, "it seems to me that we all go through these times of spiritual difficulty. For a while we're on the mountain top, and then suddenly for no apparent reason we find ourselves in the valley – out in the wilderness somewhere".

Hugh looked up. "Well, it's a relief to know that other people have the same kind of experience", he said.

"Most of us do at some time or another", I assured him, "and it seems that generally there are two reasons for it. In the first place we can get ourselves into the wilderness as a result of disobedience – you'll remember the children of Israel spent forty years in the wilderness because they refused to do God's will. It's possible for Christians to experience something similar, either through disobeying God on a specific issue or through neglecting their own spiritual welfare. Once you begin to neglect prayer and the reading of the Word, or Communion and the fellowship of God's people, the spiritual temperature drops rapidly".

He toyed with his watch strap. "I have asked God to show me if it's something I've done or something I've failed to do", he said quietly, "but I can't honestly say I've felt any definite conviction in that way".

"Well then, it may be due to the other reason", I replied. "Somewhere in Isaiah God says something like this:

'I will draw her into the wilderness and speak comfortably unto her' ".

"Actually, I think that's in Hosea", Hugh said with a faint smile, "we had to do Hosea for our finals so I know it fairly well".

"Well, at any rate, it does indicate that there are times when God Himself leads us into the wilderness, not so much because we have done wrong but in order to concentrate on some aspect of our spiritual life", I said. I reminded him of how Jesus himself was led by the Spirit into the wilderness for a process of moral development through temptation, how Philip the evangelist was led by the Spirit from the excitement of a great revival in Samaria into the loneliness of the desert at Gaza so that he could minister to another needy soul, and how Paul wrote in 2 Corinthians 1:4 about being able to comfort others because he himself had experienced the comfort of God in times of personal trouble.

Hugh pursed his lips dubiously as he stared steadily into the fire, so I tried a different line.

"When you played rugby, Hugh", I said, "were you ever dropped from the first fifteen?"

He looked up quickly and grinned. "Yes, once or twice, I suppose", he said.

"Did you always agree with the selectors?"

"You bet I didn't!"

"But what effect did it have on you?"

For a moment he looked thoughtful. "Well now", he said, "I guess the next time I played I was determined to show them they were wrong".

"So, in effect", I answered, "although being dropped was unpleasant it probably stimulated you to greater effort and in the long run improved your game". He nodded, and I went on to point out that sometimes God 'drops' us to challenge our complacency and stimulate our spiritual life.

Although it had no immediate effect, I think our conversation helped Hugh. At least the opportunity of unburdening himself and sharing his problem in prayer with another Christian made him feel less alone, and eventually he emerged from his 'deep dark valley'. As for me, the interrupted night off meant that I learned a little more about human nature than I did about Burma – and perhaps that wasn't a bad thing.

Storm over Horeb ...

Evan Harris pursed his lips and slowly blew a cloud of smoke. Through narrowed eyes he watched it writhe and curl and drift away. Outside, a pit engine shrieked and then clattered off with a long line of trucks. Grey clouds clung to the mountains as though reluctant to leave them, and the long lines of blue slate roofs on the hill slopes gleamed in the rain. For a while neither of us spoke. We were both conscious that this, our first meeting, was in some ways a trial of strength, and though neither of us would want to admit it we both knew that my presence in Evan's home was the opening gambit in an involved game of spiritual chess.

In some ways it was an odd situation. Evan Harris was a "backslider". His roots went back to the 1904 Revival, when his father had joined Horeb, the gaunt stone chapel at the end of the High Street. Through the normal process of Sunday school, Band of Hope and church choir, Evan had entered the main stream of the chapel's life, eventually following his father into the "big seat", where the deacons sat at the front. He became Secretary of the Board of Trustees and then Sunday school Superintendent, a man of growing importance.

Then Horeb was rocked by his resignation. Evan and Ruth, his wife, joined another church, but somehow he never regained his interest and gradually he drifted from his spiritual moorings.

That was where I came in. The appointment of a single minister provided Evan's new church with a good idea. "Why not ask Mrs. Harris if she would give the young man board and lodging? You never know, it might be the means of bringing Evan back!" So here I was, sitting in Evan's front room, uneasily aware of the fact that he was just as conscious as I was of the hidden reason for my presence there.

It was a situation which made me realise my need of God's wisdom. Now, as the only sound in the room was the rain rattling on the windows, I breathed a silent prayer for help. I tried to avoid anything that might arouse Evan's natural suspicion about me and began to talk as naturally as I could about ordinary things. Soon we were discussing my journey and his job, the valley and its people, our families and hobbies. These kept us going until tea time, and by then the tension had eased.

The first Sunday was rather like walking a tightrope. Evan was edgy, like a crouching dog watching every movement of a nearby cat, uncertain as to how and when he might be attacked. Sensing his feelings, I made no reference to his absence from church and suppressed any attempt at indirect "preaching". Nothing is more irritating to the odd man out than the studied casualness with which the rest of the company tell each other specially relevant bits of a sermon which they have rather conveniently just remembered. Most people would prefer to be sunk by a direct salvo than a verbal torpedo.

It was Evan who first mentioned spiritual things. He came down one supper time with several theological books. "Don't know whether they're of any use to you", he said, "But I found them upstairs amongst some things of mine in the spare room". He watched me as I looked them over, and added, "I used to do a lot of reading when I was younger". Sensing that he was willing to talk, I whispered an inward prayer for wisdom and pursued the subject. From books we went on to talk about his early days and I discovered there had been a time when he had felt a desire to enter the ministry—hence the theological books. In my eagerness to make full use of this opportunity I tried to push him further than he was willing to go and with a hastily remembered excuse he went upstairs. I had yet to learn that in dealing with men much patience is needed. The novice tries to achieve with one incision what the Great Physician knows will be a long operation.

The next opportunity came some time later, when Evan had borrowed his brother's car and offered to take me on a family outing. While Ruth and the two boys clambered over the ruins of an old Welsh castle Evan and I sat and talked.

"Evan", I said, "What made you give up the idea of entering the ministry?"

He gave me one of his quizzical looks. "It's a long story, really", he said.

I was persistent. "Tell me about it, then".

"Well, I suppose Mr. Price, the minister at Horeb, finished me. Never did get on with him, see. Whenever I suggested anything at the Trustees' meeting he always seemed to oppose me. Most difficult man he was. It all came to a head over the Sunday school Anniversary. I'd got it all arranged—lovely it was, too—then along comes Mr. High and Mighty Price . . .".

Evan's usually slow and reflective voice had found a new eloquence, and I listened to a colourful account of civil war at Horeb, in which the tyrant, Mr. H. and M. Price, aided and abetted by a band of weak-kneed yes—men on the Trustees' Board, had forced the champion of progress to resign—"on principle, you see, on principle", he said. He stared up at the ruined battlements above us as though they symbolised his own battered soul. "Even though we tried another church, I couldn't settle down after the way I'd been treated by those so-called Christians at Horeb".

I didn't get much further with him that day, and after that outburst he seemed reluctant to talk about spiritual things at all. In other ways, though, he seemed friendly and more at ease. Then suddenly I noticed a change. Evan seemed withdrawn. At first I thought he was worried over his job, but as the days went by I felt sure it was something more personal. He was not at home so much these days, and when he was at home he seemed restless, like a caged animal. Then I noticed he was avoiding me. My entry into a room seemed to be the signal for his exit. I came home one Sunday morning and went out to join him on the lawn before lunch was ready, but as I sat down in my deck chair he got out of his and went indoors. I was puzzled. Should I ask him what was wrong? Or would that make matters worse? I decided to say nothing.

The tension in the house mounted. Ruth said nothing, but I could tell she was worried. Looking back now, I suppose it would have been more helpful had I taken more initiative in the matter than I did, but I was inexperienced and uncertain as to the wisest course. A reasonable pass in Pastoral Theology doesn't make you a good minister. Only the grace of God and a good deal of hard experience can do that . . .

The crisis came one Sunday night. Tired but thankful for God's blessing on the services that day, I was about to go to my room when Evan came in. His hair was unkempt, his eyes ablaze. His tie swung half undone from a crumpled collar and his whole appearance was that of a man who had been drinking heavily. Ruth put her hand to her mouth involuntarily as he staggered towards me.

"Had a good day, Pastor?" he enquired in a mocking voice. "Any souls saved? And now shall we sing hymn number 94, 'Guide me, O thou great Jehovah'. What were the offerings like today, Mr. Jones? Oh, very good, very good indeed . . . . . ." The taunting voice rambled on, then stopped. There was an ominous lull, then Evan stepped unsteadily towards me. "I've a good mind to punch your prying nose in", he said, and pinning me to the door with one hand swung the other back to strike me. Taken completely by surprise I waited for the blow. It never came. For some reason Evan suddenly turned from me and tottered towards the kitchen. I could see that I would do no good by trying to talk to him in that mood and having made Ruth promise she would call me if she needed help I went to bed.

It was late the next day before I saw Evan again. He knocked at my door and asked if he could see me. "Sure, come in", I said, hoping this might be the opportunity I'd been waiting for. I wasn't quite prepared for what was to come.

"I've been to see Mr. Price", he said tersely.

"Mr. Price?" I couldn't hide my astonishment.

He sat down on my bed, and, clasping his hands round his knee, told me the story. Behind the facade of active service at Horeb lay an entirely different personal life and the real reason for Evan's dislike for Mr. Price was not the minister's interference in the Sunday school but the penetration of his sermons. Although he didn't know anything about Evan's unfaithfulness to his wife—Evan had taken good care about that—Mr. Price's preaching about personal holiness kept on touching a raw nerve in his Superintendent's soul. Consequently, a relatively unimportant disagreement over the Anniversary gave Evan the excuse he had been looking for. He was glad to get out of range.

But though he was out of range of Mr. Price's sermons he could not escape the Holy Spirit. Deep in his heart lay a disturbing conviction of sin, a conviction which was to be intensified by my presence in that home. "At first I was quite amused", Evan went on, "because I guessed why we had been asked to put you up. But as time went on I began to see in you what I might have been myself. I remembered my earlier ambition to become a minister and it made me realise what a sordid failure I was. Then I began to dislike you—well, not you so much as what you represented. I suppose I was like Paul kicking against the goads".

Then the affair had come to a sudden end. Humiliated and angry, Evan had lashed out—hence his attack on me the previous night—but it was the final agony of his struggle against the Spirit. By morning, like Jacob at Peniel, he could only cling to a merciful God. Somehow after what had happened the night before he couldn't face me, so he went first to see Mr. Price. He found Mr. "High and Mighty" Price a very compassionate man.

Evan rose to his feet and extended his hand toward me, and as he did so his eyes searched mine in a silent appeal for help. As I took his hand I couldn't help thinking that this was the hand that had been raised against me only a few hours before, and I marvelled at the patient grace of God.

"Let's go and talk to Ruth", I said.

Unhappy wanderer ...

"The handwriting looks familiar", I said, as I carried the morning's post into the kitchen. For a moment I stood staring at the envelope on the top of the pile, trying to work out where I had seen that sloping writing before, until a discreet cough from my wife reminded me that the easiest way of identifying it was to open the letter.

"Well, I never . . . it's from Moira . . . she wants to come and see us . . . oh dear . . . sounds as though she's in trouble . . ." My muttered exclamations gave only the barest outline of what the letter contained, but by the time we had read it over again together we knew that a fresh chapter in the saga of the unhappy wanderer was about to open – and we were likely to become some of the principle characters.

It must have been ten or more years since we had last seen Moira, though we had gleaned news of her from time to time. Even in Sunday school she had been 'in and out', coming for a few weeks and then disappearing for a month or two, only to return again and carry off the top prize in the scripture exam. Dark haired and vivacious, Moira had a zest for life which made her impatient of discipline of any kind. Then one Sunday she stayed behind after Bible class and after a long and serious talk yielded her life to Christ.

For a while she seemed steadier. With characteristic enthusiasm she set about living her Christian life and it was not long before she had brought several of her office friends into the church. I was heartened to see her coming to the weekly prayer meeting, and though she took up a lot of time with her incessant questions I was glad to see her keen interest in spiritual things. Suddenly she was missing again and when I called at her home she told me with a toss of the head that she had found a more 'spiritual' group of young people than those at our own church. In spite of the opportunities she had had in our youth activities she preferred the rather dubious fellowship to be had in one of those spiritual 'Adullums' where the discontents gather to nurse their grievances or parade their superiority.

Several months went by and Moira was back again. The 'Adullumites' had had the usual split amongst themselves and she had decided to keep to safer spiritual paths – or so she told me in her usual confident manner. I tried to help her by stressing the need for a consistent church life.

"You see, Moira", I said, "when we become Christians we become members of Christ's body, the Church, and this involves us in fellowship with the local church or assembly. Real Christianity is not a one-man-band affair, it's like playing in an orchestra – obeying the conductor and keeping in harmony with the other players. For us the 'conductor' is the Holy Spirit and the 'score' is God's word, and only as we keep together under His leadership can we begin to realise the full meaning of living the Christian life".

Moira nodded, but she wasn't listening. Instead she tucked a stray wisp of dark hair behind her ear and said, "Mind you, since I've been with this other group I've picked up some good ideas about youth work – perhaps I could come along to the next meeting of the young people's committee . . . "

During the next few months she was fairly regular in her attendance at church, but although she still had plenty to say publicly, and probably much more privately, she seemed more detached than formerly. Suddenly she was missing again. Several calls at her home and a letter failed to make any contact with her and then one Saturday morning I came face to face with her outside the local Kingdom Hall.

"I'm not joining the Jehovah's Witnesses", she said, with a characteristic toss of her head, "but I think the Lord wants me to mix with these people so that I can get to understand them"

I tried to point out the dangers of cutting herself off from Christian fellowship in this way, but Moira was adamant. This was God's will for her, she said. It was not until a month or two later that I discovered that Kingdom Hall held more than a religious interest for her. I do not believe it is wise to poke other people's fires too often, but in this case, having known Moira's spiritual background, I felt I should warn her of the dangers of this relationship. I reminded her that she had received Christ as her Lord and Saviour and that though she had let things slip spiritually yet she still belonged to Him. As gently as I could I tried to point out what the New Testament has to say about being unequally yoked to someone who did not share faith in Christ.

"Unless you can truly share the spiritual part of your life – unless you can pray together, worship together and follow Christ together – your relationship, however happy otherwise, will always lack the most important dimensions of all", I told her.

She listened quietly and promised to think over what I had said. A few days later, however, a letter in her long, sloping handwriting arrived with the news that she had decided to go ahead with her wedding plans. "Terry has decided to leave the JW's", she wrote, "and we shall probably go to the parish church. I know Terry isn't a Christian in the sense I've always understood it, but I don't believe God expects us to give up our chance of happiness for the sake of being narrow-minded. Besides I'm sure I shall be able to win Terry over to my way of thinking".

The letter was confident – as confident as the smile on Moira's pretty face as she stepped from the church porch into the sunlight on her wedding day. Flanked by her bridesmaids and leaning on her tall young bridegroom, she made a pretty picture, and the bells ringing out from the old grey Norman tower seemed to spell out her happy confidence in an almost defiant *fortissimo*. Soon after the wedding Moira and her husband moved to the Midlands, and apart from occasional snatches of news we heard nothing more of them.

Then came this letter. The handwriting was the same – but the confidence had gone. Terry had left her a year previously and she had tried to keep her two small children with her in a one-room lodging in Birmingham. Her health had given way and she had lost her job. Now she had notice to quit her room. Her own family would have nothing to do with her and there was no one in the world to turn to – unless we could help.

It was a very different Moira who eventually came back. Pale and drawn and shabbily dressed, with two restless small boys dragging at her, she was a pathetic contrast to the smiling bride for whom the bells had pealed ten years earlier. Eventually we found her a small flat and several of the church members helped her in various ways to regain a measure of independence and self-respect. Apart from a vague indication that she felt her need of spiritual help she made little reference to her spiritual situation, but one Sunday evening she made her way to the vestry.

"I know God has been speaking to me", she said, "and I realise how foolish I was to go against His will in the first place. But when you're in love it's hard to say no to your heart". She wound a piece of loose cotton round her finger and then unwound it again. Suddenly she looked at me full in the face, "Tell me", she said, in a desperately serious tone of voice, "do you think I've gone too far for God to forgive me?"

Inwardly I prayed for the right words. Quoting familiar texts to people doesn't necessarily meet their spiritual needs. "Moira", I said, "if God has been speaking to you do you really think He would do so merely to mock you?" I reminded her of the Psalmist's great words, "If thou, Lord, shouldest mark iniquities, O Lord, who shall stand? But there is forgiveness with thee . . ." Then I reminded her of God's promise to cleanse us from all unrighteousness, in 1 John 1:9. From the Scripture I tried to show her that real repentance is not sorrow over the personal consequences of sin but an awareness that we have grieved God Himself and a desire not only to be forgiven but cleansed. Gradually hope was reawakened in Moira's heart and eventually she knelt to pray in an almost inaudible whisper.

Repentance didn't solve Moira's problems overnight. She was still left to face the problem of her own loneliness and the practical problems of providing a home for her fatherless boys. Furthermore she faced many conflicts within her own self-assertive nature. She found it hard to learn obedience "through the things she suffered", but gradually through prayer and sympathetic help from her Christian friends she began to win through. The wanderer was home again, and, though the marks of the far country were still on her, there was hope in her eyes.

Next to Godliness ...

"How's that, then, Pastor?"

David Parry waved a yellow duster in the general direction of the pulpit as I entered the church. The brassware vases gleamed against the dark green velvet of the pulpit curtains and the morning sunshine was reflected in long lines of light along the even rows of highly polished pitch pine pews. The smell of polish hung in the silent building like incense, as though the caretaker had offered his own private oblation. Everything was in perfect order – even the dust particles dancing in the slanting sunlight seemed to have resolved themselves into orderly patterns – and well they might, for David had an intense dislike of any kind of disorder.

I stood beside him for a moment. "It looks fine, David", I said, answering his question, "but then it always does".

He gave the last pew a thoughtful rub with the duster. "Well, like I always says, nothing but the best is good enough for the Lord's house".

He waved the duster in a farewell gesture and hobbled off down the church, a little man with greying hair and a deeply lined face. He rarely smiled, and the eyes which looked out on the world from under their bushy grey eyebrows seemed sad and secretive. Altogether he was a quiet little man, not old by any means, but invalided out of the mine because of an accident, and grateful to the church for giving him this opportunity of doing something useful. He was deeply religious, and the opportunity to serve God in this practical way meant a great deal to him; consequently he took his duties very seriously.

Some people, in fact, thought he took himself and his work too seriously. There was the occasion when the Sunday school superintendent had come to me complaining that Mr. Parry had been unnecessarily outspoken about the state of the church after school one afternoon, and there had also been the time when I had to soothe the indignation of the bride's mother after a wedding because of David's caustic remarks about confetti in the church porch.

"And who does that David Parry think he is, then?" she demanded to know, in an ascending scale of wrath. Like many a man of few words, David could be very pointed when he did speak.

The most recent incident had found its way on to the agenda for the deacons' meeting. David had reprimanded Mrs. Jenkins for leaving dead flowers in a bucket in the church kitchen instead of in the dustbin outside. Mrs. Jenkins' tearful defence was that it had been raining but Mr. Parry dismissed the excuse contemptuously.

"Shocking, that's what it is, shocking", he said.

The words were repeated with heavy significance in the deacons' meeting. The caretaker had gone too far this time, for not only had he reduced Mrs. Jenkins to tears, that was bad enough; but he had also offended Mr. Price-Evans, the church secretary. And Mr. Price-Evans did not intend to stand for it – after all, Mrs. Jenkins was his wife's sister. The incident threatened to become a major crisis but in the end good sense prevailed. After all, as old Elisha Hughes, the genial senior deacon pointed out, why should a bunch of dead flowers threaten the life of the church? I promised to have a talk with David Parry and get him to apologise to Mrs. Jenkins, which he did, though grudgingly.

But somehow an atmosphere of strife and misunderstanding had crept into the church. Several people had left the church and others who had been keen workers in various departments were no longer active. What troubled me was that I seemed unable to put my finger on the cause of the trouble. Talking with the people concerned and praying about the matter had so far produced no real answer. It took another storm with David Parry at its centre, to clear the air.

I had been away preaching at a Convention and as the train puffed and wheezed its way through the hills a sense of foreboding gripped me. I had an awful feeling that something had gone wrong in my absence. I left the station and hurried home through the drab streets. On my way I passed the church and immediately noticed that the poster announcing the previous week's services had not been changed. That meant David Parry must be ill, for the first thing he did was to change the poster, unless . . . the other explanation did not bear thinking about.

It was not long before I found out what had happened. A letter of resignation from the young people's leader awaited me. It appeared that the young people had succeeded in getting in a crowd of down-town teenagers at their Friday night meeting. Conversations with some of them had gone on until well past midnight and because of their weariness they had decided to leave clearing up until the next day. Unfortunately for them David Parry had gone to the church early, and the sight of empty pop bottles, discarded crisp bags and cigarette ends strewn in the minor hall filled him with fury. Brandishing a scrubbing brush, he demanded that the young people get down and scrub the hall out there and then. An argument ensued in which neither side behaved very well and the result was the resignation of the caretaker plus those of the young people's leader and his deputy.

Bit by bit I pieced things together and the emerging picture was not a pretty one. What puzzled me was the reticence of the deputy youth leader. Though he and his colleague had not come particularly well out of the incident, I could understand their feelings of annoyance over the unnecessary fuss Mr. Parry had made, but I felt there was something more behind Denis Morgan's hesitation. Feeling that the key to the situation in the church might lie here I probed more deeply, and at length Denis fumbled in his inner pocket and brought out a crumpled envelope.

"It's addressed to my sister", he said softly, "but because our initials are the same I opened it by mistake, you see. Here, you'd better read it".

I took it from him and read it. It was a sordid mixture of hints about certain members of the church and other unsavoury things. It bore no signature but the handwriting was familiar. I looked up at Denis and realised that he, too, was pretty certain as to the identity of the writer.

"You'd better leave this with me", I said.

David Parry's face seemed even more lined when I called to see him and his eyes glared at me from their dark sockets with anxious appraisal. Nervously he fingered the tassels on the tablecloth, then he cleared his throat.

"I suppose you've come to see about Saturday morning", he said in a husky voice.

I nodded, and for a moment he looked at me searchingly, pursing his lips in an expression of indecision.

"Well, I'm sorry, but I can't help it. If you had seen that place you'd have felt the same. It was filthy . . . shocking. Beer bottles, cigarettes, paper and dirty footmarks everywhere".

"Didn't the young people explain that they were going to clear it up?" I asked.

"That's not the point, Pastor", he said, slapping his thigh, "they hadn't no right to leave the house of God in that state. It was awful, and I don't care how tired they were, they should have cleared up after them. In fact, they'd no business to get it in that state in the first place, it's the house of God, not a pub!"

"It wasn't beer they were drinking, you know", I said quietly, "and while we may not like the things some people do we can't just keep them outside".

"It's still the house of the Lord, even though it's the minor hall", he answered gruffly, "and people ought to respect it and keep it clean".

"Up to a point I agree with you, David", I said, "people ought to respect the house of God and keep it clean, but there's more than one kind of cleanliness, you know". I took from my pocket the letter that Denis had given me. "Do you remember writing this, David?" I asked.

He gripped the arms of his chair and his knuckles were white with tension. At first he tried to deny all knowledge of it but in the end he hung his head in a gesture of guilt.

"David", I said. "You've been concerned about keeping the church clean, and you've done a marvellous job all through the years. But you've forgotten that there are other things even more important. If you had been half as concerned about the needs of men as you are about the condition of the building, you would have not worried so much about the state of the minor hall or been petty about the mistakes of others. After all, people are far more important than buildings, and I'd rather have an untidy church where sinners are welcome than a church so perfect that people are unable to feel at home".

He lifted his head and looked at me without saying anything. I could see he was suffering great anguish yet I knew that I must touch a more vital issue. As gently as I could I showed him that he had neglected that inner, spiritual purity which was so important in God's sight. Obsessed with the outward appearance of material things he had allowed a root of bitterness to grow in his heart and spread its defiling influence to others. There was a long and painful silence as I finished talking. David sat as still as a statue, brooding darkly. He bent forward suddenly and picked up a shred of wool from the carpet.

"Is there any hope for me?" he said.

"If we confess our sins, He is faithful and just to forgive

our sins, and to cleanse us from all unrighteousness", I said. "There's always hope where God is".

The metamorphosis of Arthur Snelgrove ...

I had an odd feeling that someone was there. In the November gloom a cold, blustery wind chased a few surviving leaves across the lawn as I pressed the front door bell for the third time. There were no answering footsteps or the sudden flicker of light from the dark interior to indicate that anybody was at home, yet the feeling that someone was in the house persisted. I tried the door. It opened, but when I called out, "Anyone at home?" there was no answer. For a moment I hesitated, then spurred on by a growing sense of concern I stepped into the hall. It felt cold and deserted. Suddenly a door slammed shut upstairs. I swung round, expecting some awkward question as to my intrusion, but no-one answered my further call. "Must have been the wind", I murmured to myself.

I looked into the kitchen. There were signs of recent occupation, to judge from the half-empty bottle of milk standing on the table alongside an aluminium tea-pot and a saucerless cup. Then my eyes strayed across to the draining board and instantly a sense of alarm swept over me. There, amidst a depressing array of unwashed crockery, stood a large empty Aspirin bottle. The metal cap and a tuft of cotton wool were lying on the floor as though whoever had been using the bottle had been in a hurry.

All sense of being an intruder was lost as I searched

the house, and it was not long before I found him. He was lying on the settee in the front room, one arm trailing to the floor from under the coat with which he had covered himself, and his other hand still grasping a photo of his wife. With utter relief I discovered that he was still breathing.

It all came back to me vividly as I sat on that same settee some three weeks later and watched Mrs. Snelgrove pouring the tea. Her husband Arthur tapped his fingers ruminatively on the arm of the chair as he waited for his cup and in the meantime Micky, the Snelgroves' black and white cat, stretched luxuriously on the hearth rug and lifted a lazy paw as if registering his vote in favour of log fires. It was a scene of quiet happiness, yet only a few months ago it had been a battlefield.

I remember how Arthur and Esther Snelgrove had first come to the church. They had been deeply impressed by the consistent life and witness of a daily help and especially by the way she had faced the death of her invalid husband. They attended the funeral at our church and this led to their regular Sunday evening attendance. Several weeks later during a special evangelistic effort they both yielded their lives to Christ.

Arthur approached his conversion with the same forceful enthusiasm which characterised his work as sales manager at a local garage. He attended every meeting and was always brimming with new ideas and suggestions for improvements. In addition he was lavish with his giving. I must confess I was a little apprehensive. While I was delighted to see enthusiasm in any Christian – indeed, I often lamented the fact that so many seemed so lethargic about spiritual matters – yet I was concerned lest this fierce, almost unnatural zeal would either burn itself out quickly or else build up to a spiritual explosion. We tried, both by creating opportunities and by direct counsel, to channel and even restrain Arthur's runaway tendencies but he was impatient of any such thing.

"Look here, Pastor", he said, jerking his thumb over

his shoulder in the general direction of the garage, "down at that garage my boss is only interested in one thing – and that is, results. He doesn't ask me whether I've been 'faithful', he wants to know how many cars I've sold. And I believe it's the same with God. He wants results. The Church must learn to increase its turnover, and that means more enthusiasm, better methods and good salesmanship"

"Well, I agree with you up to a point, Arthur", I said. "We could certainly do with a lot more enthusiasm, and I agree we waste a lot of time and energy because we are not very efficient, but you know there's more to it than that. Persuading a man to buy a car or a washing machine is one thing, persuading a man that he is a sinner in need of a Saviour is far different. It's not merely a case of good salesmanship but of learning to co-operate with the Holy Spirit. Your employer is looking for results, Arthur, and that means the results of your enthusiasm and know-how; but God is looking for obedience, our obedience to His know-how".

We had many such talks, but it became clear that Arthur and his wife were impatient of the disciplines of church life. They had gathered a small circle of like-minded friends around them and although they continued to attend the Sunday services it was clear that they were drifting further from the fellowship of the church. Soon I learned that they were holding their own meetings in Arthur's home. When I called to see them they were tense but determined.

"It's just no use", Arthur said, "our spiritual life is suffering. The people at the church just don't seem to see things the way we see it. They're . . . well, I'm sorry to say it, they're dead. I mean, they're nice people and all that but they have no real enthusiasm . . . they just don't seem to care".

For a moment there was silence. I felt sick at heart, partly because I knew that Arthur's criticisms of the church were not entirely unfounded, though much exaggerated, and partly because I knew his reaction to the problem was wrong. I knew that a tangled skein of personal misunderstandings and spiritual dissatisfaction had entwined itself round the Snelgroves and would be very difficult to unravel.

"Arthur", I said, "do you believe that the majority of the people in the church are true Christians?"

He looked at me a little uncertainly, fingering the pen in his jacket pocket. "Well, of course, I do", he said, "I've never suggested they weren't".

"Well then", I said, "if that is so then they are members of Christ's Body. Granted, they may be very imperfect members and their corporate life may be far from what it ought to be, but they are still part of His Body and as such they are most precious in His sight. And in the light of that, Arthur, we ought not to reject them because they don't measure up to our idea of what they ought to be".

Arthur pulled out his pen and unscrewed the cap. "Yes, but wait a minute, Pastor", he said, "I didn't mean exactly that. What I meant was that for the sake of my own spiritual life I felt I should find fellowship elsewhere".

"And so you've decided to hold meetings in your own home?"

He nodded. "Esther and I have been round to several churches but we can't settle anywhere, so we've decided to have a few friends round for fellowship – not to start another church, of course".

I shook my head. "You know, Arthur, Jesus once said, 'Whosoever will save his life will lose it: and whosoever will lose his life for my sake shall find it', and I believe those words apply just as much to the Christian as they do to the unbeliever. If we seek to preserve our own spirituality by avoiding our responsibility to the community of Christians in which God has placed us we shall lose out in the end. When we become Christians we become members of the Body of Christ and because of this we must think in terms of the Body, not merely in terms of our own spiritual welfare. It may be that our fellow-members of the Body are not all what they should be, but unless God has shown us very definitely otherwise, our task is to be faithful in the place He has put us and seek by our prayers and the warmth of our own spiritual life and fellowship to be a blessing to His people – never forgetting that in any case we ourselves are far from what we ought to be".

My words met with no response, however, and for some months Arthur and his wife continued to hold meetings in their own home until some disagreement or other arose which brought the meetings to an end. Arthur then became enthused with the teachings and practices of some way-out sect and this eventually led to a rift between Esther and himself. Then I learned that she had left him, and it was news of his distressed condition that had brought me to the house that dark November afternoon. Fortunately there was a happy ending. Arthur and his wife were reunited, and after some time they came back into the fellowship of the church, humbler and wiser and wonderfully helpful . . .

Arthur leaned forward to put another log on the fire and then ran his finger round Micky's twitching ear. "I was reading the other day", he said slowly, "that some Christians are like butterflies when they ought to be like bees – you know, always fluttering around for their own sakes instead of seeking the good of the hive". He sat back and took his wife's hand in his own. "I guess Esther and I have had to learn that the hard way, Pastor", he said.

"We all have to learn it sometime or other, Arthur", I said, "and some of us find it harder than others. But God has a wonderful way of changing our spiritual species".

Arthur smiled. "Quite a . . . metphormosis . . . metamorsophim . . . meta . . . you know what I mean".

"Yes, I know", I said, "a change of heart".

The girl from down south ...

"The trouble with you parsons is that you've got a jaundiced view of human nature". Henry Branscombe drew ruminatively on his pipe, then picked up two faded volumes of Macaulay's *History of England,* banged them together to disturb the dust, and threw them into what he called the Shilling Bargain Box. Henry was a second-hand dealer whose shop stood next door to the church of which I was minister, and we had got to know each other pretty well, since that Shilling Bargain Box drew me like a jam pot draws a wasp.

Henry liked to think of himself as an agnostic and a Humanist, though I doubt whether his strange collection of opinions would have gained him much recognition in those spheres. Nevertheless he was an extremely likeable character, and beneath his rough-cast northern bluntness was an exceedingly warm and kind heart. I had developed quite an affection for him, and his untidy junk shop had become a kind of private tilt-yard where we engaged in friendly verbal jousts. Henry insisted that the biblical view of man was far too gloomy. Granted there were rogues here and there, but the majority of men, he insisted, were kindly and honest and only wanted better education and improved standards of living to bring out their latent qualities of goodness. He would aim his pipe accusingly at the grim battlements of the prison whose grey walls overshadowed this dreary northern town and declare emphatically, "Most of those poor creatures in there aren't basically bad, they're the victims of poverty and ignorance. Give them a better environment to live in, educate them and give them a worthwhile job to do and nearly all of them would go straight".

In vain I would point out to him that the biblical view of man was honest. "You see, Henry", I would argue, "the Bible holds the mirror up to human nature and shows it up for what it is, 'warts and all'. And whether we like it or not, the fact remains that there is an evil principle at work in human nature. Man commits sin, not merely because he lives in a bad environment, but because at heart he is a sinner. Admittedly a man's environment may either stimulate or restrain his sinful nature, but basically it's not just a man's circumstances that need changing, it's the man himself. And only God's grace through Christ can do that".

But when I had delivered myself of some line of argument like this Henry would merely shake his head, smile ruefully and then pick up some china monstrosity and blow the dust off it, as though he were getting rid of my arguments with the same casual puff.

One afternoon I called at the church to pick up something I needed, but before I reached the door Henry motioned to me from the doorway of his shop. I went over to him.

"I've got a friend of yours in the back", he said in a secretive tone.

"A friend of mine?" I couldn't think what friend of mine would want to hide in Henry's shop.

"Yes", he continued, still speaking in an undertone, "she's come from somewhere down South. Belongs to your outfit. In trouble, too. Been kicked out, poor kid. *Christians!* I tell you, mate, it's a load of eyewash. Here's a youngster that needs help, and what do they do? Sling her out on her neck! Anyway, I'll send her in to you".

The series of terse sentences followed each other like a succession of swift jabs to the chin. Henry was really worked up, I could see, so after assuring him that I'd do all I could to help I went into the church to await the girl from down South. A few minutes later the sound of footsteps in the vestibule announced her arrival, and I went out to meet her. She proved to be a rather shabbily dressed girl in her mid-twenties. Her eyes were reddened with crying but otherwise her face was pale and framed by a tangle of ill-kept dark brown hair. When she saw me she smiled wanly and then introduced herself in a hesitant southern accent.

"I'm from Pastor Lushton's church", she said, "you know, Warmfield Road".

I did a quick mental check. It was correct. Dick Lushton was at Warmfield Road. I remembered that he had recently moved to this church, which was one of three our denomination had in this fairly large town in the the home counties.

"Well, it's nice to see you", I said, "What are you doing up in this part of the world?"

She hesitated for a moment, looking around her uncertainly. "Could I talk with you privately?" she asked.

I took her into the vestry and listened while she slowly unfolded her story. Her father, it seemed, was a deacon at Warmfield Road, and she had always gone to Sunday school there, but bad company, the disgrace of an illegitimate baby and the subsequent refusal of her parents to have any more to do with her had forced her to leave home for an anonymous existence in the North.

"I can't understand my Dad", she said tearfully, "He's supposed to be a Christian, but he wouldn't have anything to do with me after what happened. Said I'd disgraced him in front of all the church. Pastor Lushton was very kind, but he couldn't do very much because my Dad was head deacon and he didn't like to interfere".

It was a sad story, and on the face of it I could understand old Henry Branscombe getting angry about the inconsistencies of so-called Christians. Then a warning note sounded in the back of my mind.

"Actually, Pastor, it wasn't that I really came to see you about. You see, I've been living in a hostel since I arrived here, and . . . well, one of the other girls must have stolen my purse last night, and now I haven't any money to pay for my week's board – you see, I have to work a week before I get any pay". She opened her handbag and after fishing about amongst an assortment of papers produced a document to verify this statement.

It was this last action that touched off the warning bell in my mind. It suggested that she didn't expect to be believed. I hesitated. Dick Lushton. Warmfield Road . . . the facts were right enough. I looked at the girl's sad face. She seemed genuinely distressed, and her story could well be true. Yet from my experience amongst people of all types I felt that there was something about this girl's story that didn't quite register. I had discovered that real need is usually most reticent, and honesty rarely feels the need of justifying itself with documents. On the other hand, I could be wrong, and I would hate to withhold help from someone in real need. Suddenly, as I hesitated, the Town Hall clock came to my aid. As it struck a quarter to three I remembered I had an appointment at three o'clock.

"Look", I said, "I have an appointment I must keep at three. Can you come back at, say, four-thirty? I'll have more time then".

She nodded, apologising for taking up my time. I watched her walk slowly down the road, and then cycled off to my appointment, feeling that at least I had a little more time to weigh the truth of her story.

The Town Hall clock had struck the half-hour before I got back to the church, but when eventually I did arrive she wasn't there. Henry Branscombe had closed his shop early, so she wasn't to be found there. Eventually I went home.

Several days later Henry called to me from his shop doorway. "That friend of yours", he began.

"What friend?" I asked..

"Why, that young girl from down South".

I laughed. "She wasn't any friend of mine!"

"What do you mean?" Henry looked startled. "She came back to me after you'd gone and told me about her stolen purse. She said you'd told her to come and ask me to lend her some money because you hadn't got enough on you, and you would pay me back later".

"Did you give her anything?" I asked.

He coloured. "Well, yes, I gave her three quid!"

I shook my head. "Henry", I said, "it's time you revised your views of human nature". I went on to tell him of my own uncertainty about the girl's story and how later I had been able to check with Dick Lushton. It was true that she had been in one of the youth groups at Warmfield Road for a while, but her father wasn't a deacon – in fact, her parents didn't attend the church. She had merely used a flimsy connection with the church to give a plausible touch to a hard luck story she had been telling in various parts of the country. In fact, the police were extremely interested in making her acquaintance.

Henry generously refused my offer to repay the three pounds, and though he would not admit that the biblical estimate of man was right I fancy that his belief in the inherent goodness of human nature had suffered something of a jolt. He tossed an odd volume of Gibbon's *Decline and Fall* into the Shilling Bargain Box.

"Makes you think", he said, reaching for his pipe.

The angel by the dustbin ...

"Well, if it isn't Mary Marchant . . . No, it can't be . . . It is, though, I'm sure it is . . . Whatever is she doing here? . . . Perhaps it isn't after all . . . "

The frustrating dialogue went on in the back of my mind, sparked off by the sight of a fellow passenger seated several rows ahead of me on the opposite side of the gangway. The shape of the head and set of the shoulders viewed from the oblique angle from which I observed them appeared uncommonly similar to those of Mary Marchant. Suddenly the object of my contemplation turned round to look for the air hostess, and the countenance that peered from behind the heavily padded seat was certainly not that of the kindly Miss Marchant. The illusion shattered, I settled back into my seat to watch the great masses of white cloud billowing up beneath us like steam from some global wash tub, and with the muffled roar of the jets in my ears slipped into a mood of cosy reminiscence.

I remembered the first time Mary Marchant had come into our church. Must have been about twenty years previous, and she would have been in her early forties then. If I remembered right, she had come from Liverpool to take up a secretarial post in the district. I don't really know why the back of her head should have been familiar because it was her face I remembered most of all. Not that she was particularly beautiful, in fact, if anything, she was rather on the plain side, but it was the expression on her face that you remembered. There was an air of wistfulness about her, as though some big disappointment in life had left her feeling she had lost the key of the door marked contentment. Mind you, she never talked about herself. Though she was courteous and friendly in a quiet way, yet she was withdrawn and never seemed to make any close personal friends. Sometimes when I caught sight of her face in the congregation I wondered what lay behind that intense, almost anxious expression.

We made several attempts to involve her in the activities of the church. Being a small church we were somewhat short of workers, and when a vacancy occurred in the Sunday school we asked her to become a teacher but she quietly declined. Then when Billy Graham came to Harringay and we were involved in counselling I asked Mary if she would volunteer, At first, she seemed as though she would be willing but asked for time to pray about it. A week or so later I asked her again but it seemed as though the shutters had come down again.

"I just couldn't do it, Pastor", she said. She hesitated, nervously clicking the clip of her handbag, as though trying to summon courage. "You see . . . " Again she paused, trying to frame a difficult sentence. "Oh, it doesn't matter . . . I'm sorry", she said, and then turned and walked out of the church.

Several weeks went by and one morning the telephone rang. Still adorned with shaving cream I lifted the receiver. "Doctor Wentworth here", said the voice at the other end. "Thought I'd let you know old Mrs. Brice has had a stroke". I thanked him for letting me know, and as quickly as possible made my way to see the old lady.

She lived in a basement flat in one of those long, anonymous London streets where crumbling three-storey houses stand in monotonous lines glowering at each other as if blaming the other side of the street for their decline in fortune. Blackie, Mrs. Brice's cat, greeted me with a plaintive miaow as I descended the basement steps and waited for me to knock and enter. As I did so I met with a surprise, for instead of the incredible muddle I was accustomed to seeing, the room had undergone a transformation. True, the faded brown wall paper, where the only pattern was caused by patches of damp, still clung desperately to the walls, and the same array of weary looking furniture was grouped around the room. But someone had obviously been busy, for the clutter of old jam jars, broken cups, left-over food and half-empty medicine bottles had disappeared from the table in the centre of the room, and the old-fashioned clothes which usually hung like dark drapes from every available chair had all been put away.

Old Mrs. Brice was lying propped up in bed looking far better than I had dared hope. And there with her back to me – perhaps that's how I remembered the back of her head –was Mary Marchant sitting by the bed, holding the old lady's hand.

The old lady couldn't talk much but she nodded in Mary's direction and whispered thickly, "Her's an angel, a perfect angel". Mary coloured slightly and shook her head.

"I'm no angel, I'm afraid", she said, "far from it".

There was a depth of feeling in the remark and I felt sure that somewhere here lay the secret of Mary Marchant's oppression. It is not often that a vital conversation takes place around a dustbin but on this occasion it was the only suitable place. I had helped Mary carry a boxful of rubbish to the bottom of the narrow strip of garden at the back of the house, and for a moment we paused by the dustbin to regain our breath. A blackened sparrow flew from the branch of a straggling apple tree and Blackie the cat crouched innocently in the long grass, which tried desperately to hide a rusting cycle frame. I crooked an arm over the clothes line".

"Mary", I said. "What's wrong with being an angel?"

She stooped and picked up a cabbage stalk and put it into the already over-flowing bin.

"Nothing at all", she said, almost abruptly, "if you can manage it".

She replaced the lid of the bin and lowered her gaze. For a while there was silence, and then slowly, almost reluctantly and yet, with a sense of relief she began to unfold an unsuspected chapter of her previous life. It is not for me to repeat the confidence of that conversation save to say that it was the story of a sad lapse from Christian standards. "And you see", she said, "though I've asked God to forgive me, and I believe He has in a way, yet I can't forgive myself. I've got the feeling that although God has forgiven me yet He would never trust me again. That's why I feel I can't take up any form of Christian service". She looked at Blackie and then away to the gaunt branch of the tree to which the sparrow, if it was the same one, had returned, then she shrugged her shoulders.

"I don't know why I've told you all this. I've never felt I could tell anyone – I suppose it's this business of Mrs. Brice that's put me off my guard. I'm sorry, I shouldn't burden you with my troubles".

"Perhaps God has given you that chance of sharing it, Mary". I said. "If you feel concerned enough about old Mrs. Brice, whom you didn't know until a couple of years ago, concerned enough to give up time and energy in looking after her, don't you think that God is concerned about you?"

"Yes, but that's different", she said, "for one thing, dear old Mrs. Brice wouldn't hurt a soul. She deserves looking after".

"That may be true", I replied, "but don't you see that God's dealings with us are not based on our deserts – if they were, none of us would have a hope. Remember what the Psalm says? "He will not always chide, neither will he keep his anger for ever. He hath not dealt with us after our sins, nor rewarded us according to our iniquities". Because the Lord Jesus bore our sins on the Cross there is forgiveness and cleansing for us".

Mary looked at me steadily. "If that is really true, why

is it that I don't feel forgiven? Why is it that I feel that God has got a kind of 'down' on me, as though He just about tolerates me but no more?"

"Perhaps it's because you have never really forgiven yourself", I said. "You know, I find that there are many Christians who are harder on themselves than God is. Maybe it's an inverted kind of pride than can never get over its own shame at doing wrong. But certainly it stems from unbelief. God declares that the blood of Christ provides cleansing from *all* unrighteousness, even the sins that hurt our ego, and He also declares that He puts our sins behind His back, never to be remembered against us any more. So God doesn't hold our past failures against us. He loves us with an everlasting love, He is full of compassion towards us, and when we truly repent of sin and seek His cleansing that's an end of the matter".

I reminded her of Peter's forgiveness after His denial of Christ, and pointed out how the grace of God persisted with Jacob after the tragic mistakes of his early life. I tried to show her that she must rest in the faithfulness of God's promise, not in her own feelings, because "He is faithful and just to forgive us". As we talked I sensed that there was a lessoning of tension in her. She gave the dustbin lid a final twist.

"Thank you", she said, "I'll think about what you've said".

Back in the house, I said goodbye to Mrs. Brice. "I'll be looking in again", I said. "Oh, and by the way, you'd better keep an eye on that angel of yours. One of these days she might start flying again!"

Prophet without honour ...

It was Sunday lunch time. I sat opposite my church secretary, Stanley Rivers, and his wife Jean. Their home was usually open to me on a Sunday and provided a welcome escape from the somewhat narrow confines of my bed-sitter.

"Quite a nice meeting this morning", I said.

Stanley looked at me over his soup spoon. "Mmmm, yes . . . quite nice".

"You don't sound too sure".

He stirred his soup meditatively. He was not only church secretary but a good friend. An older man of long experience in church life, he was a great help to a young minister and more than once I had found his counsel of great value. He never offered his opinion without being asked; he was that kind of man, so I knew I would have to press him now.

"Go on, then, what's on your mind?"

"I must confess I've been a bit troubled by some of the exercise of spiritual gifts just recently".

I nodded, feeling an inner sense of relief that the older man was expressing something of the doubt that had been nagging in my own heart. The realm of spiritual gifts was a wonderful one but like all valuable things it brought its own special responsibilities. I, too, had been a little uneasy about some of the things that had been said in interpretation of tongues and prophecy and yet I feared lest it was my own spirit that was wrong.

I shared my thoughts with Stanley now. "But you see, I've been afraid to say anything in case I should be quenching the Spirit".

He took a steaming plate of roast beef and Yorkshire pudding from Jean and quickly put it down on the table mat. "Ouch, that was hot!" he exclaimed. Then he smiled. "You can get your fingers burnt in more ways than one!"

He saw the anxiety on my face and reached for the Bible that was never far from his reach. "The thing that has concerned me has been 1 Corinthians 14:3. Look at what it says: 'But he that prophesieth, speaketh unto men to edification, and exhortation, and comfort'. Now it seems to me that one of the tests of utterances in the Spirit is whether they conform to that . . . and, quite honestly, I feel that some of the prophecies we have had just lately really haven't done so".

"Look", I said a little hesitantly, "let's be honest. You mean brother Gadby, don't you? He's worried me, too. Every time he gets up he seems to give us a good thrashing about sanctification and worldliness and so on. At first I thought the Lord was very displeased with us as a church and I was afraid in case the reservations I had were just an unwillingness to accept what the Lord was saying".

Stanley sliced through another potato. "I know how you feel, and of course it is important that we are most careful in our assessment of the gifts of the Spirit. But I believe that verse I've quoted is a good guide. It may be that the Lord has to rebuke us and to challenge our spiritual carelessness, but invariably He does so in a positive way. There always seems to be comfort alongside the exhortation. Do you remember those words in Job 5?" He turned again to his Bible. "Ah, here they are – verses 17 and 18. 'Happy is the man whom God correcteth. . .' and it goes on to say, 'For he maketh sore, and bindeth up: he woundeth, and his hands make whole'. Now that seems to be the mark of God's dealings. He never uses the rod on

His children without applying a healing balm. That's what makes me uneasy about brother Gadby. Both what he says and the manner in which he says it seem so harsh".

Stanley advised me not to take precipitate action but to lay the matter before the Lord. "If it persists, you may well have to take action", he said, "but make sure your own spirit is right before you tackle Herbert".

I must admit to a cowardly feeling of relief when Mrs. Gadby said her husband was out that evening, though I knew it was only putting off the evil day.

"Actually, I'm rather glad you've called", Mrs. Gadby said as I turned away, "I'd like a word with you".

I followed her into the house and waited while she made a cup of tea. Her hand trembled as she handed me my cup. "It's about Herbert", she said.

I was quite unprepared for what followed. Herbert, it seemed, was frequently away on weeknights. "He goes to this village about six miles away", she said, "He told me it was a house meeting and said he was just going over to help with the Bible studies. But it seems there's this young woman – her husband's left her with two small children. Herbert met her on his round and started going to the house. I thought it was just for meetings, as he said, but people have seen them in the village together and there has been talk".

"Have you talked to him about it?"

"Yes, but all he does it laugh it off and say I'm jealous. He says there's nothing in it. But there *is* something. He's . . . well, he's not the same towards me . . .and why does he have to go over there so often? They say there's hardly anyone else going to the house meeting, so why does it demand so much of his time?"

Herbert was at his most affable when I called several days later. "Do come in", he smiled, "cup of tea?" In the kitchen doorway he paused. "I've just been re-reading Bishop Ryle on 'Holiness'. Do you know it? Great stuff! Every pentecostal pastor should read it".

Remembering Paul's advice to Timothy about not rebuking an elder, I tried to be as tactful as possible in broaching the reason for my call but was not very successful. Mr. Gadby was clearly annoyed. I had no right, he said, to question the utterances of a man so much my senior in age and experience. He did not need a young man fresh from college to teach him about spiritual gifts – had been exercising them almost before I was born. He had a few more things to say about the limitations of my ministry.

It was probably not the best moment to mention the other reason for my call. On reflection I felt it would have been wiser to ask an older man, Stanley Rivers, for instance, to have tackled the whole matter but at that stage I felt it was my duty as pastor to deal with every situation in the church. Only later did I begin to learn the importance of sharing responsibility. At any rate, I felt it was now or never. "Mr. Gadby", I said when he paused for breath, "you're a great believer in holiness, aren't you?"

"Ye-es". The upward inflection on the vowel sound was like a verbal graph registering suspicious hesitance.

"Well, how far does holiness go? Is it something one merely reads and talks about in church or should it affect every area of life?"

It was not terribly tactful and it certainly had Mr. Gadby on his guard. He stood up and walked to the fireplace, nervously rattling the keys in his trousers pocket. "Look here, what are you getting at?"

It was painful for us both and my inexperience probably made it worse, but as best I could I shared with him the concern I felt over his domestic situation. What I was not prepared for was the other side of that particular story. I had yet to learn that people often only tell you as much as they think you should know and so in listening to Mrs. Gadby I had allowed my sympathy to be aroused without seeking to discover the whole truth. Now it was becoming clear that beneath the calm seas of super-spirituality the Gadby marriage was on the rocks.

Mr. Gadby was now subdued but still in control. "I can assure you there's nothing wrong in my relationship with young Mrs. Waller – why, she's more like a daughter – but the Lord has brought us together and I've found great blessing in the fellowship meetings in her home. Besides, it's given me an opportunity for ministry I don't get in our own church".

There was sufficient acid in that last remark to warn me that I was not likely to get much further. Eventually I shared my concern with Stanley Rivers but any attempt he made to help the Gadbys met with little response.

Some months later Herbert Gadby asked to see me in the vestry after the morning service. We had not seen a great deal of him during this time so the request was particularly surprising. As we sat down he was a mixture of hesitance and self-confidence. "As I'm still officially a member", he began, "I thought I ought to let you know I'm divorcing my wife. Things have become impossible and I can't take any more".

It emerged that his wife did not intend contesting the action and that he would allow her to retain the house. Grudgingly he admitted that he would be staying with Mrs. Waller. "As a paying guest, you understand", he said reassuringly.

He rose to leave but I laid a hand on his arm. I reminded him of the scriptural teaching about divorce. Was there really no hope of reconciliation? Had he really sought help in the problem? Did he really feel he could go back on the vows he had taken "for better, for worse" before God? I challenged him about the relationship with Mrs. Waller. Even if it was innocent, did it appear so to the watching world? Was it not exposing himself to temptation? I knew I was fighting a hopeless rearguard action but I tried one final argument. "Mr. Gadby", I said quietly, "do you honestly believe that what you are doing is 'perfecting holiness in the fear of the Lord?' "

For a moment he was silent. Then he stepped towards the door. "Young man", he said, "You've a great deal to learn about life". The door closed firmly behind him.

"Did you see in the *Gazette* that Herbert Gadby and

that young woman have married?" A couple of months after the divorce was finalised I was again sharing lunch with Stanley and his wife.

"How is it", I asked, "that a man who was so uncompromising about 'holiness' can do a thing like that? Remember those prophecies he used to give?"

Stanley reached for the salt. "It's a strange thing, but often a man will preach energetically against the very things that are wrong in his own life. I suppose it's a kind of inverse guilt-complex, or at least a way of varnishing over your own failures. By registering a protest against the sins of others one can sometimes delude oneself into thinking that basically all is well within".

"And it's strange, too, that a man who was so strong on 'The Word' could choose to ignore it when it really challenged his personal desires".

"Not so strange, really", said Stanley. "The more I go on the more I realise that the 'flesh does lust against the Spirit'. Theories about holiness are all very well but there *is* sometimes a conflict between what I desire as a human being and what God requires for me". He straightened a mauve anemone in the table decoration. "You see, you may be 'nearer God's heart in a garden' but most of us have to live in a jungle where nothing is quite so straightforward. So it's not theories about holiness but a living experience of the Spirit's power enabling us to obey the Word of God in a day to day walk that matters".

He reached for his Bible. "It's a case of letting Romans 8 solve the problems of Romans 7", he said turning the pages.

Jean glanced at his unfinished meal and then at the clock. "Stanley", she said with mock severity, "there's also a case for letting fruit salad and cream follow roast beef and Yorkshire, but some people don't seem to get there!"

Strife of tongues ...

It was late August. The coloured lights on the promenade swung gently against the darkening sky, and from the distant bandstand the muted sound of a military band playing popular music mingled with the murmuring swish of the evening tide sucking at the shingle. A little group of late bathers, hair lank and towels draped round their shoulders, picked their way gingerly across the pebbles, but for the most part the promenade was occupied by holiday visitors walking with the slow, almost stately gait of people who have time to spare and intend to make the most of it.

Our open air service was over but small groups of people still stood talking together. Helping one of the men to fold up the portable organ, I suddenly noticed a man on the fringe of the crowd. He was a tall man with an erect, military stance and I noticed he was wearing a light overcoat even though it was a warm evening. He had the appearance of an overseas visitor and was reading one of our leaflets with obvious interest. Somehow I sensed he wanted to talk to someone.

"Good evening", I said. "Are you on holiday?"

He smiled and extended a large hand. "Well, yes and no. I've been ill and am really on sick leave at the moment".

"I noticed you were reading our leaflet as though you were very interested", I said. "Is there any way in which I can be of help?"

Again he smiled. "I rather hope you can", he said, though probably not in the way you think. You see, I am a Christian – in fact I'm home from missionary service – but I've been ill and part of the problem is spiritual. I notice from your leaflet that yours is a Pentecostal church and that's one reason I'd like to talk to someone". He looked at his watch. "Trouble is, they're having an epilogue at the guest house, and I've promised to be there".

"Come and have coffee with us tomorrow morning", I said. We shook hands and I watched him thread his way through the meandering crowd. In spite of his height his step seemed uncertain.

His rather battered Mini pulled up outside the manse the following morning dead on time. He extricated himself from it with some difficulty and soon we were drinking our coffee in the front room.

"By the way", he said, "my name's David – David Ferguson." He stirred his coffee for the third time.

"More sugar?" I asked.

"No thanks. Just a habit – nerves, I suppose".

His eyes wandered round the room and then he nodded towards a David Shepherd print on one of the walls. "Something urgent about that", he said quickly.

"It's called 'The Last Bales' ", I said, "and it's supposed to be a harvest scene – men getting the last of the harvest in before the storm breaks".

He put his cup down. "And here am I, sitting around at the seaside when there's so much to be done on the field".

Gradually his story unfolded. A bout of malaria with complications following, personality clashes amongst the mission staff, dissatisfaction with the society's policy and a deep sense of personal inadequacy had pushed him to the edge of an emotional precipice. Only an early return home had saved him. Now he was beginning to regain physical and spiritual strength. One major problem remained, however.

"It's this business of tongues, really", he said. "This was one of the problems on the field, Some of our missionaries got caught up in the Charismatic movement and while they certainly seemed blessed they tended to adopt a superior attitude. Some of the others were very antagonistic to the whole thing and there were serious tensions amongst us. In the end it got to the stage where you were listening to each other's prayers and waiting for a "dig" one way or another. Instead of bringing us greater blessing it seemed so divisive".

He broke a biscuit in two and looked at me steadily. "Please don't think I'm getting at you – but, honestly, I feel so confused".

"Tell me more", I said.

"Well, you see, I had to admit that some of these people who had 'had the Baptism', as they called it, were certainly showing a greater effectiveness. They seemed to be more sure of God and their prayers and their general work seemed to have a new quality. On the other hand, some of them – not all of them, mind – seemed to have this, well, rather cocksure attitude. 'Spiritual snobs' I called them, and many of us found them quite irritating. In fact, whenever some of them came into staff prayers I felt quite tense and very critical".

He paused while my wife poured more coffee. "Since I've come home I've discovered a similar situation in our parish church – some very much for and some very much against this pentecostal teaching. Someone gave me *Nine O'clock in the Morning* to read – I expect you know it, it's the book about the outpouring of the Spirit amongst the episcopalians in America . . ."

I nodded and he went on.

"Then someone else gave me John Stott's little booklet on *The Baptism and Fulness of the Holy Spirit.* Since then I've had all sorts of books and booklets for and against, and I don't know where I am. On the one hand, I have to admit that the people I know who have had the experience certainly seem to have met with God, but on the other hand other people whom I respect greatly are very much opposed to the whole thing".

He clasped his fingers round his knee and leaned back in his chair, his knuckles white against the brown of his trousers. "You can see I'm pretty mixed up", he said. "In some ways I have a hunger for a deeper experience with God but the divisiveness and the spiritual conceit of some of these so-called pentecostals I find most off-putting. Anyway, I've talked far too much. I guess it's your turn. So, what have you got to say?"

I hesitated. There was an argument going on inside me. Part of me was saying "Go on, give him the answers . . . show him there are good scriptural grounds for pentecostal teaching . . . take up the challenge of the anti-penties . . . try to succeed where others have failed . . .". But another voice was saying, "This man can't take any more arguments. Resist the temptation to prove things to him; that will only feed your pride, not his soul. He has got too many crutches already, but he's still 'limping between two different opinions'. He'll have to learn to stand on his own two feet".

"Another biscuit?" I asked. He shook his head. "You know", I said, "Jesus once said He had come to bring a sword, and there are some ways in which truth is always divisive. What we sometimes call harmony can sometimes be a state of complacency, a kind of spiritual torpor, and often it is only a stiff breeze of the Spirit that succeeds in stirring us up. Truth is disturbing because it challenges us and it becomes divisive because of the way in which we react to it. But the truth itself cannot be judged by the way people react to it. There were various reactions to the preaching of the resurrection on Mars Hill – some mocked, some said they wanted to hear more and some believed – but that didn't invalidate the truth of the Gospel. So don't judge pentecostal teaching by the reactions it produces – if the truth exposes pride and prejudice it is the people, not the truth, that are at fault".

He frowned. "Yes, but . . .".

"Let me just add this", I said. "I'm not excusing the spiritual pride of people who feel they are special class of Christian. They are wrong, sadly wrong, to think like that, but doesn't mean to say that the Baptism in the Spirit, or whatever you like to call it, is not a genuine experience. The fact that someone who has recently passed their driving test has an accident does not invalidate their previous training or the test itself; it probably means they had got over-confident and failed to practise the principles they had been taught".

"Fair enough", he smiled, "but how can I really sort out the doctrinal angle?"

I looked him straight in the eyes. "You may think this odd, but this is what you should do. Get hold of all your books on the subject – *Nine O'clock* . . ., John Stott, Donald Gee, mine – if you happen to have it – all of them – and either give them away or put them in the dustbin! Close all your correspondence on the subject, don't discuss it further with anyone and don't read any more articles on the matter, either. When you've done that, get out your New Testament and read what it has to say about the Holy Spirit – read Luke 11:5-13, John chapters 14-16, the book of Acts, especially the sections which record the giving of the Spirit, and the references to the Spirit in the epistles. Don't use any commentaries but just read the scriptures and pray that the Holy Spirit will guide you into all truth. Let the New Testament itself colour your thinking and then get before the Lord in prayer. Tell Him your problem, tell Him you are willing for Him to do His own work in your life and ask Him to meet with you in His own way. Don't ask Him for a repeat performance of any one else's experience but tell Him that if the New Testament *is* the norm for today you want a genuine New Testament experience of the Spirit. And go on seeking Him until you know that He has met with you".

He grimaced. "Well, that's rather different from what I expected", he said, "but I'll give it a try – and I'll let you know how I get on".

We prayed together and he left. He waved as the Mini turned the corner but I felt he was far from satisfied. I wasn't terribly satisfied myself, either. "Don't know whether that helped him very much", I said to my wife.

I never saw him again. Then one day an air letter arrived. The writing was unfamiliar but the writer himself easily recognisable.

"I don't know whether you'll remember me", he wrote, "but we once had a long chat about the Baptism in the Spirit. I had some real problems about speaking in tongues and you suggested that I got rid of all my books on the subject and simply sought God through His Word and prayer. Well I did that – though I couldn't bring myself to put the books in a dustbin! I put them in a cardboard box and pushed them under the bed. However, nothing happened at first and I began to feel pretty frustrated. However, the more I read the scriptures themselves the more convinced I became that they described a level of spiritual reality I did not know. I did as you suggested – asked the Lord that if this really was for today He would reproduce it in His own way and time in my own life. Well, praise the Lord! I had to visit one of our outposts a couple of weeks ago and after a long journey decided to have an early night. I lay back on the bed and was thinking about the Father giving good things to His children. Then suddenly the fact that He actually was *my* Father gripped me and I began to praise Him for condescending to call Himself my Father. Then it happened! I was filled with such a sense of love for the Lord and gratitude for His goodness to me, and as I praised Him I suddenly became aware that I was speaking in other tongues – and I went on until the early hours! Next morning I woke up and wondered whether it was just my imagination but I'm glad to tell you that it wasn't. The Lord has been so much more real and I really am conscious of a new enabling in my life. I just pray that he will keep me from that spiritual pride we talked about . . .".

I put the letter down and bowed my head. "Thank you, Lord", I said, "You certainly do have Your own way of doing things".

The haunted woman ...

"You wouldn't think she was haunted", I said to myself as I walked home through the rain, "but she is".

It was a November evening. A high wind carried storm clouds across the sky and rattled the branches of skeleton-like trees. The glow of a nearby blast furnace tinted the rain-glossed roofs and the reek of heavy industry hung in the damp air. Only the occasional swish of a passing car interrupted the sound of my own footsteps. It was not a night for walking, that's probably why the prayer meeting had been down. In fact, I felt as though the damp had got into peoples' prayers. "Funny how the weather affects us", I mused. Then the face of the woman came back into focus.

Ted Barnett, the caretaker, had asked me to lock up after the meeting because he had to get home to his sick wife. Everyone had gone and I was about to turn the lights off when I noticed her. She hadn't been in the meeting but she was now standing in the vestibule, her outline just visible through the frosted glass of the inner doors.

I went towards the door. "Hello", I said, "were you looking for someone? I'm afraid they've all gone".

She turned towards me. She was a pleasant looking woman, in fact she had a motherly kind of face. She looked the kind of person you associate with a happy home and plenty of good cooking, a good natured, warm-hearted "solid" woman. Except, that is, for her eyes.

They were blue, and from the slight wrinkles round them you would have guessed they often sparkled with fun, but now they were strained as if focused on a distant object.

"Are you the pastor?" The voice was as dreamy as the eyes.

"Yes, that's right".

"Oh".

There was a long awkward pause.

"Well", I said, trying to break the tension, "is there something I can do?"

There was another long pause. Then she shrugged her shoulders. "I don't know, really". She tucked her handbag under her arm as though about to leave but seemingly an afterthought detained her: "Was Mrs. Potter in the meeting tonight?" she asked.

I nodded, thankful for a more hopeful point of conversation. "Yes, do you know her?"

"She's a neighbour".

"Oh, I see. Well you've just missed her, she went for her bus a few minutes . . .".

"Do you believe in demons?" The voice was no longer dreamy. It cut across what seemed a useful conversation path with sombre urgency.

I chose my words carefully. "The Bible does teach that evil spirits do exist, but why do you ask?"

"Mrs. Potter says I'm demon-possessed, she says I need to be exercised . . .".

"Exorcised", I corrected. "But whatever makes her say that?"

"She says I have a spirit of fear and she says it needs casting out".

I sighed inwardly. Mrs. Potter again! She was a great soul in many ways. Deeply concerned about people, always opening her home to those in need, most faithful to her church. You could be certain she would be at the prayer meeting, and when she got up to pray she would sometimes "lift" the meeting. But she had this "thing" about evil spirits. It came out in her prayers and in her conversation. At times she herself was depressed by the sheer weight of demonic power she saw in the world. More than once I had tried to remind her that Satan was a defeated enemy but she shook her head sadly: "Pastor, I don't think you really realise what we're up against", she would say.

I turned to the woman. "Would you like to tell me about it?"

She hesitated, looking round the room as though searching for hidden devices and then stared long and hard at me. Abruptly she sat down. "All right", she said.

Punctuated by long pauses, her story unfolded. It was a typical story of a comfortable, happy, mildly religious life where the seemingly secure years followed each other quite contentedly until a series of domestic time bombs exploded without warning. A son's decision to seek his fortunes abroad, the break-up of the daughter's marriage, the long illness and distressing death of the husband. Suddenly the landscape of life was leafless and littered with the debris of broken dreams.

Her attempts to find a way out had only added to her problems. The church with which she had such slender connections seemed more remote than ever. The minister had been helpful over the funeral and they had sent someone round with flowers the Sunday after, but somehow the thought of going there alone was too much, it brought back memories. Persistent depression had sent her to the doctor. He wrote a prescription and buzzed for the next patient. The garden, once her husband's pride and joy, succumbed to the swift counter-attack of weeds, the house was no longer a home but a desert island inhabited only by dark-plumed recollections. The garden fences were as isolating as the Arctic Ocean.

"In the end I went to the Spiritualist Church two or three times. They were sympathetic and at first I felt uplifted – but I always remembered my old dad telling us that it was wrong to try and get in touch with the dead. He was a Methodist local preacher, you know. Then I met Mrs. Potter in the post office and we started talking. She lives further down the road."

It was good-hearted Mrs. Potter who had shown her the first real friendship she had known for ages – but it was also Mrs. Potter who unknowingly had added yet another anxiety to her trouble-haunted mind. She had an evil spirit!

She looked pleadingly into my face. "Do you think I have an evil spirit?"

"Do you think you have"? I asked.

"I don't know, I don't know. I'm so miserable at times and I feel as though God has turned against me. Sometimes I feel as though I could scream and scream, and other times I want to just crawl into a corner and die – and yet, I know that's wrong. God must be judging me, I suppose. Perhaps Mrs. Potter is right. It must be an evil spirit . . . but I didn't know . . .".

I asked her one or two more questions about her earlier life and also probed the depth of her involvement with spiritism. So far as I could tell this did not seem to have much bearing on her state of mind.

"You know", I told her, "there are all kinds of reasons why people suffer from depression and similar illnesses. Sometimes the causes are largely physical, sometimes they are hangovers from childhood or past experiences, sometimes they are due to inner spiritual factors. Now and then, of course, they arise from the presence of evil spirits – but what you must realise is that there is no one cause that accounts for them all, and it is by no means certain that your particular situation is caused by an evil spirit".

I promised her our continual help and prayer and undertook to visit her at home. We prayed together and went our separate ways through the rain.

Seeking God's guidance in prayer, I met Mrs. Malone several times and became convinced that her problems were psychological rather than demonic in cause. I had learned one cannot make snap judgements in these matters and that much of what is called "discerning of spirits" is often not much more than guess work. That there is such a gift I knew, but I also knew that it demands a most careful walk with God and must be exercised with the utmost care.

After one distressing interview I made up my mind. Mrs. Malone was more depressed than ever. She had been taken the week before to a meeting where she had been "ministered" to. Gripped by the shoulders and energetically shaken, she had been subjected to a noisy exorcism, but the Hallelujahs ringing all round her found no echo in her own soul and she had gone home more dejected than ever. They hadn't got the answer – but then, neither had I. All my talking and praying had not succeeded, either. "Helen", I said, "you need more help than I can give you at present. There is a Christian psychiatrist I know of not far away, would you go and see him. . .?"

"A psychiatrist!" Mrs. Potter was indignant. "Pastor, you are going to undo all the good we've been doing. She was nearly delivered last time she was prayed for and now you're advising her to seek a man's help instead of God's".

"Look, Mrs. Potter'", I said, "I have a healthy distrust of psychology and psychiatry, too. I don't like many of their ideas and some of their methods of treatment I think are positively dangerous. I wouldn't send anyone to a psychiatrist unless I knew something of the man himself, and in this case I know him to be a man of integrity and moreover a sincere Christian. But let's face it – Helen Malone was not "nearly delivered" in that meeting the other night, and it's only religious make-believe to say she was. We Christians have got to have the same standards as we demand for psychiatrists – we have got to be as honest and above board as we expect them to be – and I know for a fact that neither your meetings nor my counselling have met Helen's need. Perhaps this time God is going to use a different ministry".

Mrs. Potter pursed her lips, shook her head and stalked off. Her prayer the following Tuesday night recorded her full reaction. I received more than one whiff of verbal grapeshot.

"Have you been to see Helen?" Mrs. Potter was her old self again as I met her in the street some time later.

"Yes, and she does seem quite a bit better. I notice she's been having a go at the garden, too".

"Of course it's only prayer that's done it. We've been having special prayer sessions for her at our meeting. I don't think that psychiatrist has been any help".

I refused to rise to the bait. "Yes, the Lord really has been answering our prayers, and isn't it wonderful to see Him do things in His own way. Just like Bible times – sometimes just a word, sometimes a touch, and once a mixture of spittle and clay. Fancy that – a miraculous mud-pack!"

"Anyway", I said to myself as I walked on down the street, "it doesn't matter if your name is 'mud' so long as He mixes you into His purpose and makes you the medium of His grace".

Like one of those leaves ...

The long green-tiled corridor seemed to taper away into infinity, its converging lines broken by a succession of solid brown doors adorned with heavy brass locks. My heels echoed on the stone floor and this brisk staccato seemed to amplify the difference between my noisy health and the strange silence of the wraith-like creatures who every now and then passed me, their hands clasped in front of them and their eyes distant as if beckoned by some irresistible finger. At the far end of the corridor a door slammed shut and the sound seemed to gather a deep undertone as it rolled towards me, as though it were rising from some deep well full of mystery and darkness. I walked on through the seemingly interminable green tunnel, responding to the nod of a hurrying nurse and trying to evoke something from those other silent travellers, until at length a heavy door marked "Penrith Ward" indicated that I had reached my destination. A bell shrilled as I touched the button and a few moments later the sound of a key being turned on the other side of the door announced the arrrival of the nurse who admitted me.

A bowl of pink roses brought a touch of colour into the otherwise rather bare little room next door to the Sister's office where I awaited Marie. I had been watching some of the men patients working on the flower beds on the broad lawns outside when a shuffling sound made me turn back from the window. It was Marie, escorted by two nurses. I felt a deep sense of shock as I saw her, hardly bringing myself to believe that this pathetic figure with lank dark hair falling down over a pale, expressionless face was the smart young buyer from a local store, who had also been such a keen member of our church.

The nurses led her to a chair and then left us. Marie stared at me for a moment as though trying to identify a figure from the past, and then as I took her limp hand in mine a look of recognition passed over her face and she burst into tears.

For a while I sat quietly while she wept, feeling that this would perhaps give her some relief. She sat huddled on the chintz-covered armchair opposite me rocking backwards and forwards, a pendulum of human grief gaining its momentum from continuing spasms of despair. As I watched her an awful sense of oppression seemed to descend on me, a feeling aroused not only by her misery but also by the sense of my own inadequacy. Words seemed so futile and yet silence seemed useless, too. "Oh Lord", I prayed silently, "help me to help her. Help me to get through to her somehow".

As I prayed I felt constrained to impress on her some words from the Psalms: "Like as a father pitieth his children, so the Lord pitieth them that fear him. For he knoweth our frame; he remembereth that we are dust". While I knew that merely quoting texts to people in distress was of little help, it seemed as though God had reminded me that the entrance of His word does give light. An injection of divine truth may achieve what drugs can never do. We talked for a while, but all the time I tried to bring her back to that one sentence with its great assurance of God's loving concern for His children. If only that truth could percolate into her stricken mind it might initiate a healing process.

In the weeks following I traversed the green corridor to Penrith Ward many times. Marie was showing signs of improvement and the little Scots Sister told me she was responding well to treatment and they hoped to transfer her to another ward. Then one day I called and it seemed as though Marie was right back where she had been.

"It's no good", she wept, "I'm finished. They can't help me, you can't help me, nobody can help me." She got up unsteadily from her chair and walked to the window. Outside the trees were aflame with autumn gold and a bushy-tailed squirrel ran across the lawn. "God made all that, but I can't bear to look at it any more. It's so beautiful and I'm so . . . so ugly, so useless". She slumped back in her chair and stared at me. "You see, they've tried everything: drugs, shock-treatment, everything. And none of it has done any good. The specialist saw me yesterday, but I know he can't do any more. I've let things go too far. The Chaplain came to see me, too, and now you've come, but none of you can help me, I'm just going to die . . . I wish I could die . . . like one of those leaves out there . . . just fall and disappear . . . but then God would judge me, so what's the good . . .".

Something in her tone gave me a feeling that something was at the back of this. However, just then I felt I must try to reassure her. "You're not just a leaf, Marie", I said, "you're one of God's own children and He knows you and loves you and understands how you feel". I tried to restore her confidence in the love of God. "You see, doctors and psychiatrists and ministers are all sincerely trying to help you", I said, "and in some measure they can. But whereas men try to understand you as best they can, God understands you perfectly and the Holy Spirit can reach right down to where all the cause of your trouble is and put it right– He knoweth our frame".

She seemed calmer and after we had prayed together I left, promising her that I would ask the church to pray especially for her. I was at the door of the ward when the Sister called me. "You know, Padre", she said when we were sitting in her office, "I have a feeling that there's some connection between Marie's family and her condition. I've noticed she seems more prone to these attacks of depression after they have visited her". This confirmed something that was in the back of my own mind and I determined to have a chat with Marie's people when they next visited her.

Living in London meant that Marie's parents could not visit her too frequently but on the next occasion they came I met them at the station and took them home first. They seemed a quietly respectable middle-aged couple – the father a small, neat man with a well-trimmed grey moustache and the mother a pleasant-faced woman with a gentle manner. Looking at them both as they sat on the settee in the front room of the manse, it seemed unlikely that this mild-mannered couple could have any link with their daughter's continued illness. But as we talked certain links snapped into place. I sympathised with them over the anxiety they must have felt over Marie, and as I spoke her father leaned forward, fingering one of his cuff links. "At times we feel so embarrassed about it all", he said.

"Embarrassed?" I echoed with astonishment.

He nodded. "You see, my wife and I have always taken such a strong stand on divine healing that we feel . . . well . . . *defeated* in all this. It's such a poor testimony. Of course, we've told Marie that she should get the victory over these feelings and pull herself together. We don't believe in all these drugs . . .".

I felt my temperature rising but I realised that I must keep my indignation under control. I tried a shot in the dark. "Have you ever been in hospital yourself?" I asked Marie's father.

He smiled ruefully. "Yes", he said, "two or three years ago I fell off a ladder and broke my leg. I had to go in then".

I paused. "Under traction?" I asked, and when he replied in the affirmative I pressed home the point. "Suppose that when you were under traction someone had come along and said, 'Come on, old man, pull yourself together, you musn't give in to this, you know'. What would you have said then?"

He looked at me uncertainly, "Yes, but that's different, you can't stand on a broken leg. It just won't bear your weight".

"Exactly", I said, "and in the same way a broken mind or broken nerves can't stand the weight. It's no good telling Marie to pull herself together because she can't do it, she's nothing to pull with".

"Well then, she should trust the Lord!" Marie's mother was no longer mild as the words snapped out.

I could feel myself getting angrier and I knew it would do no good at all, least of all to Marie, if I antagonised her parents.

"Look", I said, trying to keep my voice level, "I believe in divine healing, too, and I also believe that we've got to trust the Lord, but I also know that there are times when for some reason or another a Christian faces a breakdown. And when that happens it's no good condemning them because their experience doesn't fit in with our doctrinal theories; they need more than that, they need understanding and love and compassionate prayer".

I tried to show them that they were in danger of sacrificing their daughter's peace of mind on the altar of their own religious reputation, as though a broken nerve was a thing to be despised and ashamed of. Divine healing, I told them, sometimes comes through the avenue of compassionate understanding as well as through the laying on of hands.

I wouldn't like to suggest that this was the only factor involved in Marie's recovery, but the gradual change in her parents' attitude did help to speed it, and after some months she was strong enough to get her old job back again. It must have been the following year when, helping with preparing the church for the harvest festival, she picked up a spray of russet-tinted leaves.

"Just to think", she said, brushing a strand of dark hair from her forehead, "that last autumn I couldn't bear to look at the beauty God had created. And yet, it was the

Word of God that seemed to help me most of all. If it wasn't for that I think I'd still be in Penrith Ward".

I removed some tacks from my lips. "I know", I said, "it was only the Word of God that gave me the courage to walk down that green corridor sometimes".

"Old Wilkie" ...

"How do you get on with old Wilkie?" I asked between bites at one of those inevitable spam sandwiches.

Bob Black raised his eyebrows, and having taken a comforting gulp of warm tea, put his cup down on the occasional table beside him. "The man's a pain in the neck", he said abruptly.

I nodded sympathetically. I had been invited back as guest speaker to a church of which I had been the minister some years before, and now after the Saturday night service was over, Bob Black, the present minister, and I relaxed over supper at the manse. Inevitably we talked "shop" and as inevitably the subject included "old Wilkie", or, to give him his more official title, James Wilkins, Esq., Church Secretary.

"He hasn't changed much, then?" I said, "I remember when I was here . . .". The memory of old Wilkie was indeed etched sharply on my mind, and as I began to tell the story I felt as though I were living it all over again.

At that time the church had been without a minister for two or three years. A dwindling cause in a small provincial town, it had suffered from a malaise common to many such churches – senile decay. The young people had moved away to find better jobs, the old people were dying off and the middle-aged were rather too busy making themselves comfortable for the present and secure for the future. Through these difficult years, James Wilkins had borne the brunt of things. You had to give him credit for that. He it was who arranged for the speakers, saw that the church was kept clean, ran the Sunday school and generally supervised what activity there was. Then the Home Missions Department arranged an evangelistic effort in the town, which brought quite a number of new people into the church, and it was agreed that the church needed a full-time minister. The task fell on me.

I remember my first encounter with James Wilkins. As we stood together in the empty church he stroked his moustache and said, "Well, it will be a relief to hand over the reins to someone else. I don't mind telling you, it's been a hard job keeping things going through these last few years".

"I'm sure you've done a great job, Mr. Wilkins", I replied, feeling a great admiration for his faithfulness.

He shrugged in a self-deprecating gesture. "I've done the best I can", he said, flicking a speck of dust from the communion table with his glove, "but the church needs a trained minister". Then he suddenly poked me in the chest. "Look here", he said, "I know I've been in charge for the last two or three years, but you're the boss now! If I can do anything to help I will, but I want you to feel free to do what you think is best for the church".

We shook hands and went our ways, but as I walked back home from that first meeting with old Wilkie I sensed a shadow of uneasiness. "You're the boss now!" The words crept back into my mind with uncertain footsteps. What did he mean? If his idea of spiritual leadership was being "the boss" I might have an awkward man to deal with. Anyway, I told myself, he seemed very anxious to assure me of his goodwill, and with that comforting thought I reached the manse.

The first few weeks went smoothly and then one Friday night, having been detained by an urgent visit, I reached the church at about quarter to ten. The young people's fellowship was over but a group of the youngsters was gathered round the piano singing choruses. Suddenly they stopped, and in the ensuing silence I heard an irate voice telling them they had no right to be there at that time making such an awful noise. Mr. Wilkins was evidently exercising his authority! My first impulse was to step into the minor hall and intervene, but on second thoughts I decided against it. Instead I made my way to the vestry. A little later Mr. Wilkins came in. How should I tackle him about this affair? I decided to be as gentle as I could.

"Hullo, Mr. Wilkins! Have the young people finished?"

He reddened a little. "Yes", he said quietly, "they've all gone now".

"I heard them singing when I came in", I said casually, "but they seemed to stop rather suddenly. Everything all right?"

Mr. Wilkins took some keys off a hook and then turned to look at me. "Well", he said, "as a matter of fact I had a few words with them about making such a noise at this time of night. These young people have no thought at all. There's lighting and heating to pay for, as well as keeping people hanging around waiting for them to finish playing about".

"Oh, didn't they tell you I said they could stay?"

"Yes".

"And did they mention that I'd said I'd be back later?"

"Yes, but I still don't think it's good enough. They should be made to realise that they just can't go around pleasing themselves".

"Look, Mr. Wilkins", I said, as quietly as I could, "I know you're anxious to see things done properly, and I appreciate your help, but sometimes we have to stretch a point here and there. Some of these youngsters come from homes where they get no spiritual help at all, and their only chance of real Christian fellowship is here in the church. That's why I said they could stay".

Old Wilkie looked thoughtfully for a moment, then he looked me straight in the eyes. "No, I'm sorry, but I don't agree. Too much is done for these youngsters today, and they don't appreciate it any the more. I didn't have all this fuss and attention when I was their age. In my day you knew your place – and you kept it!"

I realized that further discussion was futile and I also realized that if I was to maintain my authority I would have to take a stand here and now. Old Wilkie was finding it hard not to be "the boss" any more, and if I yielded on this issue then he would expect me to yield on others. Perhaps I was over-anxious and possibly not as tactful as I might have been, but as I walked home that night I knew, quite apart from the uneasy feeling in the pit of my stomach, that things could never again be quite the same between us.

So it proved. Mr. Wilkins remained courteous and helpful, and when the first anniversary of my ministry in the church came round he paid me a gracious tribute. But his public remarks were not so influential as his private confidences, a fact we do well to remember in church life, and I began to sense amongst some of the deacons and certain of the church members a tell-tale coolness. I began to realise more and more that the issue over the young people was only a symptom of something deeper, that old Wilkie's real difficulty was over having to relinquish his long enjoyed authority. Behind the quiet courtesy was a bitter and resentful heart, and as so often happens that bitterness cast its roots into other hearts. I began to understand why the writer to the Hebrews warned his readers about the "root of bitterness" which springs up and troubles the church, causing many to be defiled. Here in my own church the poisonous weed of discontent had germinated and was growing fast. It began to manifest itself in different ways. In the deacons' meetings men who had been united became querulous, wasting time over unimportant issues and insisting on so-called matters of principle which were really nothing more nor less than means of scoring personal points. In the church itself the serpent-hiss of whispered gossip made itself heard, and people who should have known better undermined the simple trust of young converts by retailing second-hand information. It was all very genteel, of course, and the casual visitor would not have noticed anything amiss between these worshippers as they came Sunday by Sunday.

At first I tried to ignore it, hoping that it would die a natural death, but when it persisted I tried a new approach. I endeavoured to give Mr. Wilkins greater recognition, including him as much as I could, even in matters which were really outside his responsibility, but this failed, too.

At last I tried to grasp the nettle. Calling at his home, I tried the man-to-man approach, hoping that an honest talk might clear any misunderstanding between us. Even this failed, however, because old Wilkie insisted that as far as he was concerned nothing was amiss. It was all imagination on my part, he assured me. If only he would come out from behind that mask of politeness and face the facts, unpleasant though they were! All I could do now was to leave the matter with God. In the end it took a stormy deacons' meeting, at which he was forced by an unexpected issue to declare himself, to bring things into the open. The storm cleared the air and eased the tensions which had been building up within the church. No longer able to pretend that nothing was wrong, Mr. Wilkins apologised, but somehow things were never the same. Every now and then came verbal rumblings that warned me that the volcanic fires of personal ambition were not yet extinct in old Wilkie.

"It's a sad thing", I mused, gazing into the fire, "when a man of great experience and ability lets his own feelings come between him and the purpose of God and won't admit that something is wrong. Better by far to be honest about things, even if it hurts".

Suddenly I realized I had been doing all the talking, and seeing the amused look on Bob Black's face I hastened to apologise. Bob waved his arm in a reassuring arc. "No, no", he said, "I'm not laughing at that. You see, the funny thing is that when I had my last do with old Wilkie he told me that he always got on all right with you!" And seeing the unbelieving look on my face Bob laughed all the more.

"Absence makes the heart grow fonder", he said.

Question 9 ...

Question nine was the awkward one. It made me get up from my desk and walk over to the window in search of inspiration. Outside, a blustery wind plucked the blossom from the almond tree in the front garden and scattered it like a shower of pink snow amongst the drooping tulips. The unexpected greyness of the morning offered no help. I returned to my desk and picked up the form again. All the others were easily answered but question nine was a problem. "What", it asked, "is your candid opinion of the candidate's suitability for missionary work?"

What could I honestly say to that? Probably I was the one who knew Veronica best of all. It was in this very room that she had come to Christ. My mind went back to the Friday evening she had come to see me. She had sat in the old arm chair opposite me asking question after question. She was an art student at the time and she had a keen sense of the dramatic. I could see her now spreading her hands in an expansive gesture and widening her eyes and saying: "If you can prove to me that Jesus is the Son of God I will become a Christian".

I remembered shaking my head and saying, "But it isn't quite so easy as that. God doesn't make a philosophical bargain with us, promising to answer all our questions in the hope of persuading us to accept Him. In fact, God requires repentance, not simply intellectual assent". I had gone on to point out that Jesus Himself had said, "If any man will do his will, he shall know of the doctrine, whether it be of God, or whether I speak of myself", so that in the spiritual realm intellectual proof follows personal obedience.

The discussion had gone on for a long time before Veronica finally saw that to be a Christian was not simply accepting a certain collection of beliefs about God but rather repenting of personal sin and turning in faith to Christ as Saviour and Lord. It was late that evening when she eventually yielded her life to Christ.

The first few weeks after her conversion things seemed to go well for her. Her intellectual difficulties, as she called them, were apparently resolved and she entered into the fellowship of the church with characteristic enthusiasm. She persuaded several of her fellow art students to attend the church and frequently could be seen in the midst of an ardent discussion group after the services, her own elegant gestures adding force to the points she made.

Then one evening the phone rang. It was Veronica. She was, she said, devastated. An older Christian, who should have known better, had let her down badly. It had made her re-examine the implications of Christianity, she said. Surely something was wrong with its "moral dynamic"? I pointed out that the church was not a club for saintly perfectionists but a hospital where sinners are brought back to spiritual and moral health. But because of the far-reaching effects of sin in our lives the process is a long and painful one. It was only through the grace of God, I said, that we did not fall more often. I stressed that this did not excuse sin in the Christian but it did explain it.

A couple of weeks later the phone went again. Veronica had another problem. A fellow-student had lent her a book on Philosophy in which the basis of Christian belief had been challenged. It was, she said, a shattering experience. She was now an agnostic. Again a long conversation followed in which we tried to pick up the pieces of her shattered faith and put them together again. When I saw her the following Sunday she smiled thankfully. "I feel as though I've been through the dark night of the soul", she said in a half whisper. I was glad to know it, though as Bob Peters, the college chaplain, said when I mentioned it to him, it must have been an arctic night, it was so short.

It's a wonder they didn't make Veronica the patron saint of the GPO, because she must have made a substantial contribution to its revenue through the time she spent on her telephone. Huge crises seemed to engulf her like a succession of emotional high tides and she would invariably telephone an urgent SOS. It became obvious that she was craving attention and that these appeals for help arose from more than purely spiritual matters. In the end I made myself less available, endeavouring at the same time to provide the necessary spiritual help for her in the fellowship of others in the church. But until she left the town several years later she remained unstable, the graph of her spiritual temperature soaring and plunging like that of a feverish patient.

So what could I say? Veronica wanted to be a missionary. I could picture the enthusiasm with which she would apply. But was she really reliable enough? I hated to stand in her light, yet I had to tell the truth. It might hurt her temporarily but it would be kinder in the long run. Slowly, as gently as I could, I wrote my candid opinion. And when the society's magazine arrived months later I saw with an inward pang that Veronica's name was not on the list of new candidates.

It must have been six or seven years later that an air letter from the USA lay on the front door mat one morning, "Who on earth is this from?" I muttered as I picked it up. Inside were eight or nine pages of elegant handwriting and as I turned quickly to the last page to see who the writer was, the name "Veronica" leapt from the page. She was on her way home from a far eastern country for her first furlough and wondered whether she could visit us while she was in England. The letter told of how dejected she had been after her rejection by the missionary society, but also how God had used the chance remark of another Christian to jerk her out of her self pity and challenged her to face the truth about herself. "I can see now", she wrote, "that my rejection was one of the 'all things' that worked together for my good. Had I gone to the field when I wanted to I would probably have spoiled my own life and the lives of others as well. It would have been tragic". The letter went on to say that she had eventually been accepted by another society and had now completed her first term on the field.

It was obvious that Veronica had undergone a transformation. And when at length she did visit us this first impression was confirmed. Granted, the old animation was still there and the same fluent gestures gave vivid impact to her description of her life as a missionary, but there was also a new quality, an air of quiet certainty, of dependability. She packed away her slides and projector and came back to the manse for supper. For a while she concentrated on her meal, then suddenly she looked up.

"Do you remember once saying something to me about the Church being a hospital not a club?"

I nodded.

"Well, you know, I've often thought about it since. When I first became a Christian I thought everything would be cut and dried, you know, no loose ends and no failures". Her fork looped a delicate loop and she went on. "I suppose I had to learn that life is untidy, that sin has created so much disorder that it takes time to unravel the tangle". The fork glinted as it performed another, more complex manoevre. "I suppose I was in too much of a hurry – I'm afraid I even treated the Bible like a promise box, expecting an appropriate text to jump out at me every time I opened it. But I've learned . . . I've learned . . . " Her voice trailed away as her fork swooped on another piece of tomato.

"You're not the only one who has learned", I said. "Quite honestly, I had more or less written you off as a failure. It's funny, really, but in my estimate of you I had done the very thing I told you not to do – I'd forgotten that God takes time over His dealings with us. In a way, it's a bit like the story of John Mark. Paul wouldn't have any more to do with him after he'd turned back from that first missionary journey. And yet in the end he had to write to Timothy and say 'Bring Mark with you, for he is profitable to me', or words to that effect".

She smiled. "It's a good thing God is the Chief Consultant in the hospital".

"Yes", I said as I sipped my tea, "and it's a good thing He doesn't take too much notice of question nine".

Secret assignment ...

"Forasmuch as it hath pleased Almighty God of His great mercy to take unto Himself the soul of our dear brother here departed, we therefore commit his body to the ground . . . " The words of the Committal fought for survival amidst the almost indecent roar of life from outside the cemetery. The staccato clanking of goods trucks shunting on a nearby track, the defiant roar of an accelerating sports car and the thousand and one sounds of the busy streets came stalking down through the fir trees and weed-infested crosses as though the living were trying to haunt the dead.

I closed the book and looked down at the bronze name plate on the cheap coffin. "Albert Fennimore. Aged 89 years" was the simple inscription. Pale spring sunshine spilled into the upturned trumpets of a bunch of daffodils lying on the grey city earth. There was only one bunch of flowers for Albert, and only one mourner. Mrs Simms, a small plump woman with a kindly face, fingered the top button of her overcoat.

"Poor old chap", she murmured, "he was no trouble – not to me, anyway. Had his funny ways, of course, but then, we're none of us perfect, are we?" I nodded assent and then, as the figure of the grave digger loomed from behind a nearby tombstone, we turned and made our way back to the small terraced house where Albert had lodged with Mrs Simms.

Sitting on the arm of a chair and sipping the welcome cup of tea Mrs Simms had made, I surveyed the pathetic collection of Albert's earthly possessions. His cloth cap and woollen scarf still hung from a hook on the back of the door, partially hiding the walking stick that had supported his tottering legs on his last walks. Apart from a crumpled suit and a couple of grubby shirts there was little else. I picked up a faded sepia photograph from the mantelpiece.

"His mother", Mrs Simms confided.

"Quite a good-looking woman", I said, noting the fine features of a face framed by dark, well-groomed hair in the piled-up manner beloved by the Victorians.

"Came from a good family, he did", said Mrs Simms. "He used to tell me about his early days. They was business people, it seems. Lived in Norfolk somewhere. But they lost all their money during the war – the first one, of course".

The terse sentences etched a simple picture of Albert's life and I found myself reflecting on the strangeness of life. I looked again at the photograph and imagined the excitement of that well-to-do home when Albert was born; the champagne, the congratulations, the gentle smile of this fine-looking mother as she cradled her first-born in her arms. Who would have thought that that much-loved baby, ensconced in lacy frills, would end his days in cloth-capped anonymity with a solitary bunch of daffodils on his grave?

"All his papers are in that right hand drawer". Mrs Simms' matter of fact voice broke across my reverie. I had promised her I would help sort out his things and so I crossed the room to open the old chest of drawers. It contained very little. Half a dozen old letters, a box containing his war medals, half a candle, an assortment of buttons, some miscellaneous papers and a dog-eared Post Office savings book. I opened the latter and scanned its contents. It contained the usual assortment of deposits and withdrawals, mostly quite small sums. On the last page, however, there was an interesting entry. It was a withdrawal of £100 and it was dated some six months prior to his death. A quick calculation told me that this withdrawal had just about cleaned up the account. When we had finished sorting out the rest of Albert's things I went home and the first thing I looked for was my diary for the previous year. There, on a Friday in September, was the cryptic note: "Meet Albert, 2.30 at Library". That Friday in September came several days after the date in Albert's savings book.

I remembered with a twinge of conscience that I had felt irritated when the phone rang earlier that week. It was the third time it had rung in half an hour and I was in the middle of an address for a ministers' fraternal. My irritation had not been eased by the fact that it was Albert's high-pitched tremulous voice at the other end. Albert could keep you for ages when he got going. This time, fortunately, he was more to the point, though somewhat mysterious.

"Pastor, I want to meet you privately", he said, "somewhere where we won't be seen". Intrigued, I agreed to meet him outside the Public Library that Friday.

"Not that the Public Library is very private", I muttered to myself as I put the phone down.

The Town Hall clock had just struck the half hour as I threaded my way through the crowded streets to the Library. Albert was already standing by the steps. Although a mellow September sun lingered lovingly on the red brilliance of the geraniums in the window boxes of the otherwise smoke-blackened Library building, Albert was prepared for Winter. His cloth cap was pulled well down, his woollen scarf was tucked round his throat and his hands were thrust deep into the pockets of his shabby fawn raincoat. He stood half facing the Library steps as though he did not wish to be seen and yet still wanted to observe the passers-by.

"Hullo, Albert", I said cheerfully as I reached him, but he laid his finger against his lips and shook his head as though I had committed a serious blunder. Then, having looked up and down the street, he motioned to me to follow him up the steps.

We passed through the swing doors and into the reading room. Here Albert paused and surveyed the occupants as though looking for a secret agent. Apparently there wasn't one amongst the silent band of elderly readers, for he led me on into the library itself. No word passed between us as he led me slowly between the long rows of shelves to the far end of the room, but then suddenly he spoke: "This'll do", he said in a hoarse whisper. We were at a deserted corner beside some shelves marked 'Over-sized Books' and Albert was peering this way and that to see whether we were being observed. When he was quite sure no-one was watching he dug into his raincoat pocket and brought out a package wrapped in newspaper. He held it out to me.

"I want you to take this, Pastor, and send it to the missionaries", he said. "You'll know where to send it better than I do", he went on, and then looking at me sternly he added, "Don't open it, mind, and don't tell anyone anything about it! I don't want anyone to know anything about it and I don't want my name in the paper'"

I hesitated. Holding the mysterious parcel in this deserted corner of the Library made me feel like a man involved in espionage. I didn't know what the package contained – there was no way of telling from the feel of it – but if it was something very valuable could the old chap afford to give it away?

"Look, Albert", I began, "are you sure this is all right? I mean . . . "

Again he held his fore-finger on his lips. "It's all above board, Pastor", he whispered, "but it's my own private affair, see? I've been planning to do this for a long time and as things are I might not have much more time now, so I'm doing it while I've got the chance. Don't say any more about it". With that he tapped me on the shoulder like a veteran dismissing a recruit. "We'd better leave this place separately", he said. "You go first!"

Obediently I had fulfilled his wishes, and until this day I had had no knowledge of what was in the parcel. Now it seemed pretty obvious that Albert, sensing maybe that he had not much time left, had scraped together his savings and given them for the missionary cause.

A couple of weeks after the funeral I had a letter from Albert's younger brother. He was sorry, he said, that he couldn't come to the funeral, but could I tell him whether Albert had left any Will? It didn't take me long to reply.

"Your brother", I wrote, "left no Will, in fact he left hardly anything. He did draw his savings from the Post Office a few months ago, but he never told anyone what he did with the money".

Which was perfectly true. Mind you, I've got a good idea where it went, and I know where the final account is kept. But recording angels don't disclose things like that.

Decline and fall ...

Sunlight streamed through the windows of the church hall, throwing brilliant pools of light amongst the circular groups of children in their Sunday school classes. Reg Barnes, the superintendent, and I stood near the platform watching the progress of the school. Through the warm, drowsy atmosphere of a summer's afternoon the teachers' voices rose and fell in a regular flow, punctuated now and then by the scraping of a chair or the sudden flurry of excited voices harshly whispering "Miss!" in answer to a question. Reg Barnes nodded towards a class of ten year olds. "Mrs. Parker's class engrossed as usual", he said admiringly. "She really knows how to put it over".

I followed his gaze to where Mrs. Parker was talking animatedly to her class. The small ring of boys seemed to be almost on top of her as they leaned forward absorbed in the lesson. She was indeed a fine teacher, not only because she knew how to put it over but also because she was able to win the respect and trust of her class. You could see them lingering behind to talk to her after Sunday school, and sometimes she would have the whole pack of them to tea and then bring them back to the Sunday evening service, where they would sit in a well behaved row between her and her husband. She called them "my lads" and was a second mother to many of them.

Reg nodded to me significantly. "She lives for those boys, you know", he said. It was a remark I was to remember.

One Sunday in the early autumn Mrs. Parker asked to have a word with me after the evening service. As she sat down in the vestry she fingered her necklace nervously, as though a little unsure of herself.

"Well, I thought I ought to explain what has happened", she said. "You see, my sister's husband has recently died, leaving her with a small baby to cope with, and I have suggested she comes to stay with us for a while. The thing is, I'm afraid I shall be unable to take my class for a while – of course, it will only be for a few weeks but I thought I should let you know. I've already seen Mr. Barnes about it".

The request seemed reasonable enough, but somehow I had that tell-tale feeling of uneasiness blinking like a warning light in the back of my mind. I suggested that perhaps her husband would take over the class temporarily, so as not to break the valuable contacts they had made with the boys, but she said they had already talked this over and he felt he couldn't take it on.

She was very reassuring, however.

"I shall miss the boys so much", she said with a smile, "but it will only be for a few weeks and then I'll be back with them again". I dismissed my misgivings and turned my thoughts to more pressing problems.

It was Reg Barnes who touched off that warning signal again one Sunday afternoon. He nudged me with his elbow – always the sign that he was about to impart some special information – and inclining his head towards my ear whispered confidentially, "You know, it's ten weeks and there's no sign of Mrs. Parker coming back". I hadn't realised how quickly the time had passed, but Reg's words reminded me that the Parkers had not been so regular in their attendance at the Sunday services just recently, either.

"I think I'll call on them during the week, Reg", I said.

On my way to the prayer meeting the following Tuesday I called at the Parkers' home. Sid Parker was oiling the front gate when I arrived.

"I expect you've come to see the Missus", he said with a slightly uncertain smile. I'll give her a shout".

Inside their small, quietly furnished council house Mrs. Parker motioned me to sit down and then sat down herself, or rather perched herself on the edge of the settee. "I expect you're wondering why I haven't been back to Sunday school?" she said.

I looked beyond her to where her husband stood in the kitchen doorway wiping the oil from his hands. "Well, partly that", I said, "but I've missed you both from church just recently".

Sid went on wiping his hands, obviously leaving his wife to be spokesman. Mrs. Parker meanwhile straightened the engagement ring on a rather chubby finger, gazing at the small diamond as though it were a kind of private oracle. Then, as though the gem had inspired her, she looked up quickly. "Well, quite honestly, Pastor", she said, "things have been a bit difficult just lately". She went on to explain how her sister's stay had put a strain on their rather modest income and how she had taken a part-time job to help. And, of course, there was the baby. Caring for it had taken up a lot of their time. "My sister isn't the world's best at coping at any time, and what with her husband's death and everything, we felt we had to help, for the poor little mite's sake above all".

I nodded. "Yes, of course", I said. "And I think that as Christians we ought to be willing to take responsibility in these situations. Sometimes we can get so tied up in 'spiritual' activities that we become like the Levite and the priest in the Lord's parable about the good Samaritan".

Sid Parker was looking more relaxed. "That's just what I've always maintained, Pastor", he said, "after all, religion is more than rushing off to meetings all the time".

"You're right up to a point, Sid", I said, "although the New Testament does warn us not to neglect 'the assembling of ourselves together' – and after all, it is in the fellowship and service of the local church that our spiritual life finds its fullest expression". I paused and looked over at Mrs. Parker. "Still, now that your sister and the baby have gone back to Manchester, I guess you'll be wanting to get back to your lads", I said.

There was a slightly awkward silence in which Mrs. Parker fingered her engagement ring again and her husband disappeared into the kitchen. Then she cleared her throat. "To tell you the truth, Pastor", she said slowly, "I won't be able to come back just yet". She went on to explain that having been able to secure her part-time job had meant that they had been able to get a few extras for the home which otherwise would have been impossible. "So we thought", she concluded, "that while I still had the job we would try to replace some of our furniture. It will only be for a few months and then I could perhaps come back to Sunday school – that's if you'll have me back, of course".

I assured her that we would always value her as a teacher, but I also tried to point out that her absence would mean severing, perhaps for good, some valuable contacts with her boys. "I can understand how you feel about improving your home and there's no sin in that, of course", I said, "but as Christians we are called to seek first the kingdom of God and His righteousness, and in making decisions of this kind we need to be sure that we are doing His will".

For a few weeks the Parkers were much more regular in their attendance at the services, but as time went on we saw less of them. When I called at their home some time later it had been transformed. New carpets and furniture had given it a sophisticated look. But when I complimented them on it and sounded Mrs. Parker about her class now that this objective had been reached she smiled understandingly, but shook her head.

"Much as I would love to come back, Pastor", she said, "I won't be able to for a while. You see, my boss has been ill and they've asked me to do Sunday work – only for a month or two, until he can come back. I wasn't going to, but really our old car needed replacing and we felt the extra money would help us get something a bit better". She saw the dubious look on my face and hurried on. "You know, we felt we could do so much good with a bigger car – getting elderly people to church and so on . . ."

Reg Barnes and I stood on the church steps watching the last of the Sunday school children leave when the notes of a two-tone car horn arrested our attention. We looked up to see the Parkers glide by in their shining new car. We responded to their friendly waves and then I felt Reg's elbow digging into my ribs.

"I'm afraid we won't see Mrs. Parker back any more", he said. "I can't understand it".

"Do you remember once saying to me that Mrs Parker lived for her boys, Reg?" I asked him. He nodded. "Well, I believe that that was where the trouble began", I said. "You see, she lived for her class rather than for Christ Himself, and when anything – even the work of God itself – takes His place then we are on dangerous ground. It seems to me that Mrs Parker's spiritual life depended on her activity in Christian service rather than on her personal walk with God Himself, and when that activity was removed for a while her spiritual life was deprived of its stimulus and so it shrivelled. She lived for her class until the baby took its place, and then when the baby was gone her job moved into the vacuum. I suppose you could say she loved Christ because she served Him, rather than served Him because she loved Him . . . "

Reg looked at me a little quizzically, as though he wasn't too sure about that last remark. Then he stooped down to pick up a discarded text card, and as he straightened up his elbow probed for my fifth rib.

"I reckon you've got something there", he said.

The geezer ...

"Oops . . . Sorry, Pastor . . . There's a geezer to see you . . ." In one breath apology and information exploded from young Sandy Wallis as we collided near the vestry door.

"Sandy! I've told you before about dashing about the place", I said sternly. "And another thing, we do not refer to people as 'geezers'. They're people, men and women, ladies and gentlemen, not geezers!"

A few minutes later Sandy re-appeared and with a rather unceremonious "He's here, Pastor" left me alone with my visitor. The man was short and stocky in build, with a balding head that made him look rather older than he probably was. I judged that he was in his late forties. There was a nervousness about his manner as he sat down opposite me. His small grey eyes avoided mine and darted about the room as though looking for an easy exit. He took a rather grubby handkerchief from the breast pocket of his crumpled grey suit, mopped his somewhat flushed face and then, clearing his throat, said, "I'm in terrible trouble . . . terrible trouble. In fact, I came here to finish everything – I've been up to the Witch's Pinnacle but at the last minute my nerve failed me".

I found myself looking at his shoes. Anyone who had been on Witch's Pinnacle, especially during the recent spell of very wet weather we had been having, would almost certainly have had tell-tale chalk marks on his shoes, and though I hated to be suspicious I had learned from a long experience of listening to plausible stories that it helped if one could sometimes verify some of the facts. As it happened, my visitor's wrinkled and muddy brown shoes neither confirmed nor denied his story, so I gave him the benefit of the doubt.

"Tell me about it", I said.

For a moment he was silent. He ran a tobacco-stained finger round the inside of his grimy white collar and then leaning forward, with his elbows resting on his knees and his chin cupped in his hands, he stared at the floor. Still in this position and without looking at me he drew in a deep breath and began to unfold his story.

He was, it seemed, a research chemist working for some large establishment in the North-East. He had been engaged to be married for some years, but because his widowed mother was dependent upon him he had never felt free to get married. Then about three months previously his mother had died, and the shock and distress this had caused him had been followed by an even greater blow. His fiancee, just at the time when marriage seemed at last possible, had returned his ring and refused to see him any more. He lost all interest in life, his work suffered, and the final blow had come two days ago when his firm sacked him.

"I don't blame them, really" he said, still gazing at the floor, "I'm afraid I'd just let myself go, and I couldn't concentrate on anything. This morning I made up my mind to finish it all. I caught the train and came here. Then I walked up to Witch's Pinnacle, intending to throw myself over. But when I got there I couldn't bring myself to do it".

He paused. The only sound was the rhythmic ticking of the vestry clock, and in the stillness I pictured this lonely little man, forlorn and wind-swept, standing on Witch's Pinnacle and looking down at the swirling grey waters of the North Sea foaming round the savage rocks three hundred feet below.

More often than not a man in trouble needs a sympathetic listener rather than a talkative adviser, and so I listened as patiently as I could while Harvey Blake traced the crossed lines of his troubled life. At the same time I tried to point him beyond the narrow confines of his own confusion to the wisdom and grace of God. All the time, however, a niggling uncertainty turned restlessly at the back of my mind. At length he rose to go. By this time it was late, and so I asked him where he proposed staying the night.

He hesitated, his eyes avoiding mine, and then murmured, "Well, I don't really know. You see, I didn't bother to take more than my train fare this morning, because . . . well, I didn't think I'd need it any more".

The captain in charge of the nearby Church Army hostel, a very good friend of mine, willingly helped out with the accommodation problem and I left Harvey in his care, having arranged to see him again the following morning. He turned up punctually for the appointment and, though prone to wander back through the tortuous paths of his troubles, seemed a little less strained than he had been. I promised to help him find a job and lodgings, and he seemed pathetically grateful.

"You don't know what this means to me, sir", he said, "but one day I shall hope to repay you".

In the event the lodgings proved an easier problem than the job. Bob Walsh, a retired city missioner, and his wife gladly welcomed him into their home, and I felt happy in the knowledge that they would care for him spiritually as well as physically. In the meantime I had been in contact with a friend who had a large business in the town, and he was able to offer a job.

"Of course", I explained to Harvey, "it's not a highly paid job, but at least it will give you a chance to pay your way while you are trying to find something more suitable". He thanked me profusely, and went on his way.

A couple of days later he called to see me. "How's the job going?" I asked him.

He ran his finger round the inside of his collar and cleared his throat. "Well, to be honest with you, I didn't feel I could face another inside job. I didn't like to tell you at the time, but since my trouble I must have developed a kind of claustrophobia, and I just can't face another indoor job . . ."

He began to wander into a long description of his 'trouble', as he now called it, but eventually I managed to get him into a more positive frame of mind. Together we scanned the local paper for likely jobs. "How about this one?" I asked, pointing to an advert for a van driver. Harvey looked dubious but agreed to try for it.

Towards the end of the week I met him as he wandered down the High Street. Before I could say a word he said, "I mustn't stay now, I've got to get to the Labour Exchange". I asked him about the van driver's job.

"It would have been all right, but the hours were too long". Seeing the uncertain look on my face he added, "Well, I wouldn't have been able to get to the weeknight meetings at church, and I feel I do so need spiritual help".

Once again I gave him the benefit of the doubt, but an uneasy feeling about him persisted at the back of my mind. It wasn't eased when I met Mr. Walsh later the same day. There was a shrewd gleam in the old missioner's eyes as he stroked his well-trimmed moustache and said in his clipped Scots accent, "I'm no' so sure about yon man. The other night he kneeled down in our front room and gave his heart to the Lord. I thought he was genuine at the time, but I'm beginning to wonder. Och well, we must give the laddie a chance, I guess".

Hearing no more for a couple of days I called at the Walsh's. Harvey was sitting by the fire, writing pad on knee, and a cup of tea on the table beside him. "Just writing after another job", he said a little hastily.

"How did you get on at the Labour Exchange?" I asked.

Again he seemed to avoid looking at me. "Well, they could only offer me a job at a market gardener's place, but when I went after it I found it involved heavy lifting, and you see, with my trouble . . ."

"Harvey", I said firmly, "I'm beginning to wonder whether you really want a job. You find something wrong with every one you go for. It's very nice sitting in Mrs. Walsh's front room drinking tea, but you owe it to the Walsh's as much as to yourself to find a job and pay your own way, especially if you have become a Christian".

Once again he fingered his collar nervously and cleared his throat. The job he was writing for this time was just what he wanted, he assured me, and he felt sure he stood a good chance of getting it. "I won't let you down, Pastor", he said.

Late the following Friday night Mr. Walsh phoned. "Have you seen Mr. Blake?" he asked. I hadn't. "Well, his bed hasn't been slept in last night, and we've seen nothing of him all day", Mr. Walsh reported. And he didn't sleep in that bed again, for none of us ever saw or heard anything more of Harvey Blake.

"Och well, we tried our best to help him", Mr. Walsh commented when we talked it over a few days later. For myself, I wondered . . .

All in a day's work ...

"And Lord, please help Steve and Marion . . . I wonder why Wally Hampton wasn't there again last night, that's two Sundays he's been missing . . . Lord, Thou knowest how Steve has been so tempted and tried . . . I wish next door wouldn't let that blessed dog bark so much first thing in the morning . . . and Thou knowest, Lord, that Marion . . . funny how old Wilkie and John Harper were talking so intimately last night after the meeting, hope they're not cooking something up for the deacons' meeting . . . Lord, Thou knowest . . . Lord, please help me to overcome these wandering thoughts, I can't seem to get anywhere this morning . . .".

It was one of those mornings. In the end I managed to rein in my galloping thoughts by reading afresh the passage of Scripture that I had already read absent-mindedly twice before, but by the time I was composed and able really to concentrate Mrs. Grange, my landlady, was knocking on the door with the morning cup of tea. She paused in the doorway, looking beyond me to where my open Bible lay on the arm of the chair.

"It must be wonderful to be a Pastor", she said.

"Wonderful?" I echoed in a slightly incredulous tone.

"Well yes", she answered, "You know what I mean, it must be wonderful to be able to do nothing else but God's work all day. I wish I had the time to pray and read the Bible like you do. Sometimes I find it very hard.

It must be wonderful to be able to be . . . well, you know what I mean, *an expert*".

I shook my head. "You know, Mrs. Grange", I said, "it isn't as easy as that. I find it hard to pray sometimes, just like you do. Take this morning for instance . . .".

But Mrs. Grange wasn't having it.

"Oh, go on with you", she said. "It's easy for you, you've got the time". And before I could reply she sniffed and exclaimed "Here! the bacon's burning!" and fled to the kitchen.

Barking dogs, befuddled prayers and burnt bacon. Not an auspicious start to the day! I sat at the rickety table which served me for a desk and tackled the morning's mail. Apart from a very welcome letter from home there wasn't much: a bill from the printers, three circular letters and a postcard reminding me that I had agreed to speak at a Womens' Bright Hour the following Thursday. The morning passed quickly as I got down to preparing my weekly Bible Study. At first I wished I'd never started the series on Colossians, but now I was committed to it I had to get on with it, and in the end the study began to take shape. I was so absorbed in it that I didn't hear the knock on the door that announced the arrival of a red-faced and breathless Billy Hogan.

"Mum's sent me round to tell you that they've taken Maureen into hospital", he puffed.

I sensed in Billy the tension that was hanging over his home and I could picture his mother fighting her feelings as the ambulance drove off and she had to turn back into the house to try to prepare the dinner for the rest of her large family.

"Tell Mother I'll look in to see Maureen as soon as I can and then I'll look in and let her know how she is. Oh, and tell her not to worry", I added, at the same time reminding myself that that was easier said than done.

A faint smile flickered over Maureen's face as I entered the ward. I thought how frail and tense she looked, like a lost child in a busy, antiseptic world of pain and birth, life and (sometimes) death. A serious heart condition had cast a shadow over the prospect of her first child and the anxiety over this, added to the sense of bewilderment in her strange new surroundings, accounted for the nervous way in which she kept bunching the bed cover in her thin fingers. We sat and talked, and I tried to assure her of God's unfailing love and care. We read together from Psalm 56: "What time I am afraid, I will trust in thee", and then I waited while she scribbled a short note for me to take to her mother.

Half an hour later, having delivered the note and given a first-hand report to Maureen's mother, I cycled on to the general hospital to visit old Mr. Gregory. When I reached his bed I could see he was not likely to last much longer. I leaned over and spoke close to his ear but the only response was a momentary interruption of the otherwise rhythmic sighing of his laboured breathing. For a while I sat by his bed, conscious of the strange contrast between the busy activity all around me and the quiet oblivion of this old man. The rattling of instruments on a trolley, the swift footsteps of hurrying nurses, the distant clattering of crockery being washed, a plaintive cry of "Nurse!" from a nearby bed, the slow shuffling walk of an elderly man on his way to the bathroom and from outside the sound of an ambulance arriving: these were the audible evidence of Man's continual struggle with sickness and death. But for this little old man with the sunken cheeks and the grey hair the struggle was almost over. Soon this sighing breath would cease, the flickering blue vein in his temple would stop throbbing, and they would wheel him away. But not his soul. Old David Gregory had walked with God for most of his 87 years, and if there were no relatives to sit by him in his last hours he would not worry unduly for, to quote his words to me on a previous visit, "The Lord is with me, Pastor, and I'm not afraid to go".

Leaving the hospital, I called in at the poster writer's

to leave my copy for the Easter poster. As usual, Barry Marsden was squinting through a cloud of cigarette smoke at some delicate silk-screen work.

"Easter poster?" he queried when at last he did look up.

I nodded and then we chatted over the layout.

"By the way", Barry said, "I've finished a nice job for the Youth for Christ rally". He reached for a folder and showed me a sample of the leaflet. "See, black for sin, red for the blood of Christ, and white for purity. How's that?"

"Fine", I said, "and I'm glad you get the symbolism. But you need to know more than that, you know!"

Barry shrugged and reached for his mug of half-cold tea. "I'm only interested in the format, I guess. As long as it looks all right that's all that worries me".

"And that's all that worries a lot of people", I thought to myself as I made my way down the stairs, "but life is more than good format, it's the message that counts".

With this on my mind I rode off to my next call. Soon I was seated in the front room of Mrs. Denham's council house, trying to sort out some tangled lines. Mrs. Denham was convinced that the Secretary of the Women's Fellowship had deliberately tried to ridicule her by calling out her birthday on the wrong week. All my suggestions to the contrary failed to allay her dark suspicions and in the end I could only point her to the Scripture: "If thy brother shall trespass against thee, go and tell him his fault between thee and him alone . . .". Mrs. Denham looked dubious. I fancied she was wondering whether the matter was that important after all.

Out into the sunshine again and down through the narrow streets of the older part of the town to where old Mrs. Maynard lived. The little room with its dark wallpaper and faded photographs smelt strongly of paraffin fumes and mothballs, but there was always a kindly welcome. I watched her sinuous hand tremble as she poured the tea and wondered how much longer she would be able to keep her jealously-guarded independence. We drank our tea in silence, the occasional gurgle of the oil-heater the only sound in this drab room.

"If it wasn't for the Lord, I don't know what I would do, Pastor", Mrs. Maynard said. "I've no one left now that Mary has gone abroad". She took a sip of her tea. "Why doesn't the Lord take me home? I've nothing to live for now, and I've asked Him to take me. Why doesn't He?"

What can you say to a weary old lady in her loneliness? I promised to arrange for some of the church visitors to look in more often but I knew that what she really wanted was to "go home". I reminded her of the Psalmist's words, "My times are in thy hands", and tried to point her again to the loving wisdom and tender care of the God who is "touched by the feelings of our infirmities".

Eventually I arrived home for tea, but soon afterwards was on my way out again to conduct the prayer meeting. After the meeting Hugh Williams wanted to ask my advice about a new post he had been offered, Mrs. Sharpe wanted a word about her grandson who was in trouble with the police, and George Mathers wondered if I could spare a minute to discuss the positioning of speakers in the minor hall. It was nearly ten before I arrived home for supper and I had not been in long before Maureen's husband called to let me know that she had given birth to a son and they were both all right.

Mrs. Grange was in the hall as I made my way to my room.

"Had a good day, Pastor?" she asked.

I paused for a moment. Today I had studied the Word of God, had been privileged to share that Word with people facing fear and misunderstanding, loneliness and worry, ignorance of the truth and uncertainty about personal decisions; had stood on the threshold of a new life and paused in the valley of the shadow of death.

"Yes, thank you, Mrs. Grange", I said, "a **very** good day!"

The firstborn ...

The imperative clang of an ambulance bell jerked me out of a doze. Through narrowed eyes I peered at the clock on the waiting room wall and noticed with surprise that the hands pointed to five minutes to nine. It was almost an hour since the other husbands had left the hospital, and since then the only sounds to disturb me had been an occasional flurry of squeaky footsteps on the polished floor and the swish of a starched uniform as a nurse hurried past. It had been a tiring day and I was quite glad of the chance to sit back and relax while waiting for Douglas. His young wife Jane had been taken into hospital two days before, but it was only this evening that the boy had been born, and as I had promised to run Douglas to the hospital as soon as he had news I found myself alone in this quiet oak-panelled waiting room.

I picked up the well-thumbed copy of *The London Illustrated News* which had slipped from my lap during my impromptu doze and tried to take an interest in the sepia pictures of the launching of an oil tanker two years previously. Then I caught the sound of footsteps. This time it was Douglas! I rose to meet him, a not very original quip about his entry into fatherhood on my lips, but the quip fell into the abyss of unspoken thoughts, for one look at his face told me something was wrong. Neither of us spoke as we made our way through the revolving doors to the car, but once in the car Douglas seemed to crumple and his shoulders shook in silent anguish. Then a half-choked groan escaped his lips.

"Is it . . . Jane?" I asked quietly.

He shook his head. "No", he said, between long pauses as he struggled for control of himself, "it's . . . the baby . . . something's . . . wrong with it . . . "

Something was indeed wrong. When I called at the hospital the next day the Sister in charge of Jane's ward looked serious. "Aye, the poor wee mite is badly deformed", she said, "and the Doctor says he'll probably never walk". She paused, and then in a hesitant undertone she added, "It would have been a mercy if the good Lord had taken him". But my problem was how to relate the goodness and mercy of the Lord to the sadness that had overwhelmed the pale-faced girl with the dark-rimmed eyes who was waiting for me in the ward.

"Perhaps there's some purpose in it", she whispered.

I hesitated. It's the easiest thing in the world to quote Romans 8:28 when someone else is facing trouble, but what can you say to a young mother whose eagerly awaited firstborn turns out to be a helpless little deformed thing? One thing I was certain about, Jane wouldn't find much help from me if I proceeded to give her an exposition of my views on the problem of suffering. Instead I tried as best I could to point her away from the "Why?" to the "How?".

"Jane", I said, "I don't know why this has happened, any more than you do, and just now this isn't the most important question we have to answer, What you and Douglas need is to know how to face this situation".

I picked up the Bible lying on her locker and turned to 2 Corinthians 12:9 and read the words of Paul: " 'And he said unto me, My grace is sufficient for thee: for my strength is made perfect in weakness'. God doesn't promise to answer all our problems", I found myself saying, as much to myself as Jane, "But He does promise us His presence in our trials. And it's only because of His strength and love that we can find courage and grace to help us face the sorrows and disappointments of life".

We prayed together and then I left, pausing only for a moment at the door to wave farewell, and as I looked back at this young mother with the wan smile and the sad heart I felt oppressed by the sorrow that seemed to encircle human life and by the pathetic inadequacy of human words to alleviate that sorrow. But as I walked the long corridors of that hospital my heart found some relief from that same letter to the Corinthians: "The father of our Lord Jesus Christ, the father of mercies, and" – how did it go? – "the God of all comfort; who comforteth us in all our tribulations . . . " The words rose like a gentle fountain amidst the oppressive heat of my spirit, and I prayed as I walked, commending Douglas and Jane to the God of comfort.

"Douglas wasn't in again this morning", my wife said as she put my plate before me. We were holding the inevitable after-church stocktaking common to many a manse. Several weeks had gone by, and Jane and the baby were now at home. They had brought the baby to church and asked that we would pray that God would heal him, but since that morning we had not seen them. At first we attributed their absence to the inevitable upheaval in a home that follows the arrival of a baby, but we were now beginning to wonder whether there might not be other reasons. I decided to visit them the following evening.

"Jane's gone round to her mother's", Douglas explained, hastily removing the nappies which festooned the fireguard. We sat down in the easy chairs and I explained the reason for my call.

"Well, you know what it is with a new baby", he said, "and Jane hasn't been too good since she came out of hospital". He gave an apologetic laugh. "I never realised a baby made such a lot of work. I've been trying to give her a bit of extra help, but as soon as we've settled down we'll be back at church".

It all sounded very reasonable, but somehow I felt it

wasn't the whole truth. Douglas was too honest to be very successful at hiding his real thoughts, and it was this that made me direct in my dealings with him.

"Douglas", I said firmly, "I've got a feeling that there's some other reason why you've been staying away from church".

For a moment there was an awkward silence. Douglas stared into the fire, slowly rubbing the tips of his fingers together. Then he leaned back in the chair.

"Well Pastor", he said, clearing his throat, "to be honest with you, there is something".

Slowly the truth unfolded. In the first place he was hurt and puzzled by the mystery of it all. An edge of resentment sharpened the tone of his voice as he spoke. "After all, I know we're not perfect, but we have always tried to follow the Lord. Why should it happen to us? Other people live any-old-how and nothing seems to happen to them". He leaned forward to replace a piece of coal that had fallen from the fire and then turned to look at me, the flickering firelight gleaming in his questioning eyes.

"Have you ever read the eleventh chapter of Hebrews?" I asked him. He nodded. "Well, have you ever noticed the great contrast between the first and second parts of the chapter?"

I asked him to pass me the Bible on the sideboard and together we looked at the chapter. "You see", I said, pointing at verse 35, "right up to the first part of this verse it's mainly a record of great triumphs and great deliverances, but at this point there's a sudden change: 'others were tortured . . . had trial of cruel mockings . . . were stoned . . . tempted . . . destitute, afflicted, tormented . . . '. Now the people in this last part were no less men and women of godliness and faith than the people in the first part – they 'all obtained a good report'. But you see that didn't necessarily guarantee them immunity from trouble". I tried to show him that faith in God and obedience to Him do not automatically ensure that we shall be free from trouble and sorrow, but that sometimes through our disappointments and difficulties God works out some greater purpose in our lives. The Lord Jesus Himself shared our experience of sorrow in order that He might be a faithful and merciful High Priest, able to understand our infirmities because He had experienced them personally. In a similar way God sometimes led His people through sorrow so that they might be able to minister to the needs of others, comforting them with the comfort they themselves had received from God, as Paul puts it in 2 Corinthians 1:4. "You know, Douglas", I said, "the very way in which you face this trial might be the means of proving to your neighbours the reality of the Christian faith".

"But surely", Douglas countered, "when we brought the baby to church and asked you to pray that God would heal him, God would have answered our prayers if He really cared about us?"

"Douglas", I answered after a long pause, "there are lots of things I can't answer. God's ways are past finding out". I reminded him of the story of the washing of the disciples' feet and how Peter objected to what Jesus was doing, and how Jesus replied, "What I am doing you do not know now, but afterwards you will understand". "You see", I said, "there are times when we simply have to trust God without insisting on explanations. Like Job we have to be willing to say, 'Though he slay me, yet will I trust him' ".

They weren't very clever words, but I think they helped. At any rate, Douglas and Jane made their way slowly back to the high road of faith, and as the time went by we saw the development of their spiritual life. In some ways, the very demands made on them by their helpless firstborn seemed to draw out from them hidden reserves of love and courage, and gradually the hurt and resentment were transmuted into the fine gold of patient endurance by the alchemy of God's grace.

One day when little Douglas was about two years old

I looked in to see how Jane and Douglas were. We tip-toed into the small boy's bedroom and stood looking down at him. "You know, Pastor", Douglas said, "he's brought us nearer to each other and nearer to God than we've ever been".

I nodded. "Strange, isn't it", I remarked, "but when he was first born there was a text I felt I just couldn't quote to you, and yet I suppose you'd be the first ones to quote it now".

"What's that?" Jane asked with a smile, "Romans 8:28?"